THE
MAKING OF AMERICA
SERIES

THE
WHITE MOUNTAINS
ALPS OF NEW ENGLAND

The jagged peak of Mount Adams rises majestically above the Mount Washington Carriage Road in this nineteenth century engraving from Picturesque America.

THE
MAKING OF AMERICA
SERIES

THE
WHITE MOUNTAINS
ALPS OF NEW ENGLAND

RANDALL H. BENNETT

ARCADIA

Published by Arcadia Publishing,
an imprint of Tempus Publishing, Inc.
2 Cumberland Street
Charleston, SC 29401

Printed in Great Britain.

Library of Congress Catalog Card Number: 2003103127

For all general information contact Arcadia Publishing at:
Telephone 843-853-2070
Fax 843-853-0044
E-Mail sales@arcadiapublishing.com

For customer service and orders:
Toll-Free 1-888-313-2665

Visit us on the Internet at http://www.arcadiapublishing.com

Front cover: *Willey Brook Bridge on the Portland and Ogdensburg Railroad, Crawford Notch, 1879.*

CONTENTS

ACKNOWLEDGMENTS

This book is a sequel to and expansion of my previous Arcadia title on the White Mountains, first published in 1994 and reprinted several times. Most of the images in the present work are from my own collection, but for the generous loan of certain other photographs I would like to thank Stanley Howe, Bill Robertson, the Bethel Historical Society, and George and Danna Nickerson. I would especially like to thank Danna Nickerson and Stanley Howe for proofreading the text and for making suggestions regarding the book's content and focus.

Littleton, New Hampshire, became an important center of manufacturing and commercial activity before 1900. The rooftop cupola and columned portico of Thayer's Hotel can be seen on the left side of Main Street.

INTRODUCTION

The White Mountains occupy a special place in the history of America. Because of their proximity to the North Atlantic coast and their consequent accessibility to people of the earliest settled portion of the United States, these picturesque highlands have achieved a notoriety disproportionate to their height and relatively compact geographic area. Ancient hills these are, like the rest of the Appalachian Mountains of which they form a part. Spread across northern New Hampshire and spilling into western Maine, the glacier-worn peaks of the White Mountains are dominated by the storm-swept cone of Mount Washington and are home to the largest alpine area east of the Rocky Mountains and south of Canada.

The story of the "Alps of New England"—a term made popular by Victorian era writers—is a fascinating and often melodramatic chronicle of the interrelationship between a people and a natural area. Once viewed as a symbol of the vanishing American wilderness, the White Mountains can scarcely be thought of as "wild" today. Civilization has tamed this haunting and memorable slice of backcountry, where outlet mall shopping in the "Mount Washington Valley" now competes with hiking, skiing, and scenery-watching for those visiting North Conway and other tourist towns in the eastern half of the region.

Nearly two centuries ago, the sublime grandeur of this "Switzerland of America" drew well-heeled vacationers northward, first by coach and later by railroad car. The famous Willey Disaster of 1826, in which a landslide destroyed an entire family while sparing their mountain home, supplied America with one of its first major tourist attractions, and provided the inspiration for early White Mountain art and literature. Attracted to the area through the paintings of Thomas Cole, William Henry Bartlett, and Henry Cheever Pratt, as well as the writings of Nathaniel Hawthorne, Lucy Larcom, and John Greenleaf Whittier, tourists found the White Mountain tour a powerful tonic for a rapidly industrializing society. The phenomenal development of the region as a resort destination was largely due to the railroads, which by the 1870s had pushed their way into the very heart of the mountains and up the western side of Mount Washington. The "Golden Age"

Glacial potholes created by swirling, sand-laden waters are found in streams throughout the White Mountains. Here a family poses above the Shelburne Basins.

of White Mountain tourism saw the rustic taverns of such mountain men as Eleazer Rosebrook and Ethan Allen Crawford replaced with sprawling grand hotels that could accommodate up to 600 guests at a time and whose gracious hospitality matched any then available in the urban centers of Boston, New York, and Philadelphia.

By the late nineteenth century lumber barons moved in, buying up vast tracts of forest land and building logging railroads into the most isolated corners of the region. In a matter of just a few years, clearcutting and rampant forest fires decimated the land, and streams were left choked with debris. A lack of vegetation on the steep mountainsides allowed rainwater to flow unchecked into some of New England's major river systems: the Saco, Merrimack, Connecticut, and Androscoggin. Downstream, flooded manufacturing centers were forced to close, further alarming a public that was increasingly outraged by such an obvious misuse of resources. After a number of false starts, the federal government finally took action in 1911 by passing the "Weeks Act," which set in motion the creation of the White Mountain National Forest. Containing nearly 800,000 acres—an area a little larger than Rhode Island—in New Hampshire and Maine, the Forest is managed to provide a variety of uses, including outdoor recreation, the preservation of wildlife habitat, and the harvesting of timber.

No longer the exclusive domain of the wealthy, the White Mountains have become a year-round visitor destination, and today some of northern New England's most popular ski resorts can be found both inside the White

Mountain National Forest and on private lands just beyond its boundaries. Likewise, many people still choose to live and work here on a permanent basis, where they are reminded each day that with an appreciation of these spectacular surroundings comes a responsibility for their proper stewardship, lest the mistakes of the past be repeated. An enchanting land of sweeping valleys, steep-sided notches, and granite-capped peaks, the White Mountains remain a place where legendary vistas and celebrated heights combine to delight and inspire visitors in ways that are timeless.

Randall H. Bennett

North America's first passenger aerial tramway was built on Cannon Mountain in 1937-1938. Over seven million passengers were carried on the original tram, which was replaced in 1980.

9

1. Mountain Geography and Geology

The White Mountain region is crowned by a 70-mile segment of the Appalachian mountain chain that rises prominently above the forests, lakes, and rivers of northern New Hampshire and northwestern Maine. Encompassing the 770,000-acre White Mountain National Forest, this fabled district—America's first tourist playground—boasts the highest peaks east of the Mississippi and north of the Carolinas, including the celebrated 6,288-foot Mount Washington. Anchoring the western boundary of these mountains, which have a southwest-to-northeast orientation, is 4,802-foot Mount Moosilauke, the highest point of land between Franconia Notch and the Connecticut River. At the far eastern end, where the rugged Mahoosuc Range drops dramatically into the scenic gorge of Grafton Notch, is Old Speck, a 4,170-foot behemoth that ranks as the third highest mountain in Maine. In all, the White Mountain region covers some 1,200 square miles, an area that by tradition also embraces the spectacular Alpine scenery of Dixville Notch in the far northern reaches of New Hampshire. Of the nearly 100 mountain peaks in that state and in adjacent parts of Maine, 49 rise 4,000 feet or more above sea level. In addition, the headwaters of four major river systems—the Saco, Merrimack, Connecticut, and Androscoggin—are contained within this distinctive area of northern New England.

The White Mountains are a place of legend and, indeed, of superlatives, but they admittedly fall far short of being the loftiest mountains in America. This lack of elevation is more than made up for in age, for these splendid New England peaks are some of the most venerable mountains in the world. In fact, geologists now estimate that the boulder-strewn "alpine zones" of the Presidential and Franconia Ranges, located above 4,800 feet, contain sand, silt, and clay that began to accumulate at the bottom of a shallow inland sea approximately 500 million years ago.

The permanency suggested by the towering heights of the White Mountains conceals the power behind the natural forces sculpting this unique landscape for millions of years, and that still act upon it today. Volcanic activity, stream erosion, compressional uplift, and the freezing and thawing of frost are just a few of the forces that, over countless eons, have transformed this region and given it its present character. Surprisingly, the term "Granite Hills," used for so long to identify these mountains, is actually a misnomer. A large number of the higher peaks in the White Mountains are made up of schist, gneiss (pronounced "nice"), and quartzite—tough, erosion-resistant metamorphic rocks created by tremendous heat and pressure.

Scientists familiar with the types of rock formations found in these mountains believe some 450 million years ago a chain of volcanoes existed in what is now the Gulf of Maine, and vast quantities of volcanic debris were carried by westward-flowing streams to the ancient sea that then existed here. Although the great weight of accumulated sand and ash, estimated to be as much as 5,000 feet thick in places, caused the bottom of this shallow sea basin to sink, it eventually filled up and a dry plain a few thousand feet in elevation took its place. Far beneath this plain, layers of sedimentary rocks were slowly being compressed under enormous pressure into sandstones, shales, and impure limestones.

An extended period of faulting and folding began about 375 million years ago, largely as the result of the North American plate colliding with those of Europe and Africa. Molten rock seething up from far below the earth's surface also

The White Mountains include the highest peaks east of the Mississippi and north of the Carolinas. The snow-covered Presidential Range was observed by mariners off the coast of Maine as early as the 1520s.

pushed sections of the vast plain skyward, and in some places flowed freely across the land, producing the numerous outcroppings of granite and other igneous rocks, including pegmatite, that are so common in the central and western White Mountains. The resulting landscape resembled the present-day folded Appalachian Mountains of Pennsylvania, West Virginia, and North Carolina. Further compressional stresses caused dynamic physical and chemical changes to underlying layers of material; in some cases, extreme pressure caused individual crystals in these metamorphic rocks to fuse together, leaving few crevices in which water or ice could later accumulate to break them down. As this period drew to a close, the forces of erosion began to alter the land, washing away some of the less resistant rocks and causing V-shaped valleys to form.

About 300 million years ago, a second major intrusion of molten rock into the existing metamorphic rocks took place. Transformed over millions of years into a relatively resistant granite, this series of rocks is evident today in the broad shoulder of Cannon Mountain where the famous Old Man of the Mountain is located. Over the next 200 million years, a mass of rock 7 miles thick was worn away by the forces of water, wind, frost, and ice. Removed at a rate of about 1.9 feet every 10,000 years, this material was slowly transported westward into the Catskill Mountains and areas further west and south, leaving the entire elevation of northern New England a rolling plain somewhere close to sea level. The few surviving areas of high ground may have topped out at no more than 1,300 feet. Geologists working in the White Mountains have identified remnants of this plain in the great flat stretches of the Alpine Garden and Bigelow Lawn, on the eastern side of Mount Washington at the base of its summit cone. The Gulfside Trail on that same mountain takes advantage of this relatively level upland surface.

The final lifting of this region to its present 5,000-foot altitude, a process that took several million years, resulted in a series of sharp-peaked mountains located where the major summits of the White Mountains exist today. As before, streams began to erode deeply into the now higher surface, cutting into granitic rocks that were more easily broken down than the tough schists of the Presidential Range. Tributary streams developed rapidly on the valley sides, producing waterfalls much higher than those in the region now. Gradually, the White Mountains took on an appearance resembling what we see today. It now remained for the final great molding of the land to take place.

For unknown reasons, some two million years ago changes in the earth's climate brought about colder temperatures and a marked increase in snowfall. The resulting Ice Age involved at least four different stages when glaciers advanced and retreated over much of North America. In the White Mountains, great rivers of ice and snow carved their way over the highest mountaintops, scouring ledges, rounding summits, and deepening valleys. In Franconia, Crawford, and Pinkham Notches in New Hampshire, and Evans Notch in Maine, the glaciers deepened the V-shaped valleys and converted them into awe-inspiring U-shaped troughs. Even before the main ice sheet covered this region,

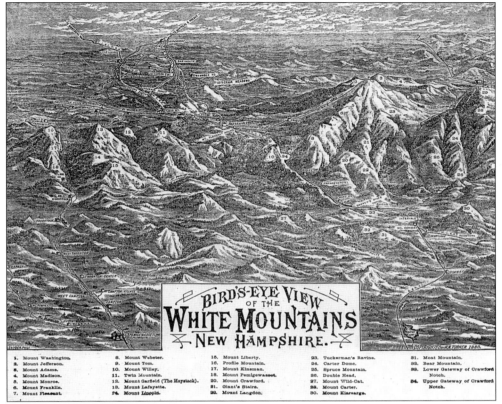

BIRD'S-EYE VIEW OF THE
WHITE MOUNTAINS
NEW HAMPSHIRE.

1. Mount Washington.	8. Mount Webster.	15. Mount Liberty.	23. Tuckerman's Ravine.	31. Moat Mountain.
2. Mount Jefferson.	9. Mount Tom.	16. Profile Mountain.	24. Carter Dome.	32. Bear Mountain.
3. Mount Adams.	10. Mount Willey.	17. Mount Kinsman.	25. Spruce Mountain.	33. Lower Gateway of Crawford Notch.
4. Mount Madison.	11. Twin Mountain.	18. Mount Pemigewasset.	26. Double Head.	
5. Mount Monroe.	12. Mount Garfield (The Haystack).	20. Mount Crawford.	27. Mount Wild-Cat.	34. Upper Gateway of Crawford Notch.
6. Mount Franklin.	13. Mount Lafayette.	21. Giant's Stairs.	28. Mount Carter.	
7. Mount Pleasant.	14. Mount Lincoln.	22. Mount Langdon.	30. Mount Kiarsarge.	

A layer of ice a mile thick covered the White Mountains during the last Ice Age. Weathering and erosion continue to shape the region's character.

prevailing southwesterly winds dumped huge amounts of snow on the eastern and northern sides of the mountains. This eventually created small glacial tongues whose downward movement plucked soil and boulders away, cutting out great amphitheater-like canyons. These unique glacial "cirques" with their steep headwalls and broad floors are evidenced in Tuckerman and Huntington Ravines on the eastern flank of Mount Washington, as well as in the Great Gulf and King Ravine to the north. Around 12,000 years ago, the last of these enormous sheets of ice, which once topped the Presidentials by a mile or more, began to melt away to leave the landscape much as we now see it.

Despite thousands of years of continual erosion and numerous landslides (the most famous of which destroyed the Willey family in Crawford Notch in 1826), the evidence of continental glaciation remains conspicuous throughout the White Mountains. Huge scratches, or "striae," were created as rocks dragged along the bottom of the ice flows, and are still visible on many ledges. These gouges or grooves trend in a northwest to southeast direction, which was the route of the glaciers. Perhaps the most interesting remnants from this great

13

MT. WASHINGTON FROM PINKHAM NOTCH.

The forces of glacial activity carved out Tuckerman and Huntington Ravines on Mount Washington. Huge boulders plucked from the mountain were deposited many miles away.

wearing down of the landscape are the glacial "erratics," massive boulders that were ripped away from ledges far to the north and deposited by the slow-moving ice around the region. The Madison Boulder, near Conway, is believed to be one of the largest erratics in the United States; it is 83 feet long, 37 feet broad, and 23 feet high, and weighs an estimated 7,650 tons. The Glen Boulder, an immense rock perched on a prominent shoulder of Mount Washington, is another erratic that has long been a familiar landmark for travelers through Pinkham Notch.

No commentary dealing with the geology and geography of the White Mountains would be complete without mentioning the "whiteness" of the White Mountains. Just when these peaks received this designation cannot be determined exactly, but the term "white hill" was used as early as 1642 by Governor John Winthrop when speaking of Darby Field's pioneering ascent of Mount Washington. Frederick W. Kilbourne, whose 1916 book *Chronicles of the White Mountains* remains the most authoritative history of the region, inclined toward the "rock theory." It states that the mountains were defined "from their white or whitish-gray aspect when seen from a distance, which appearance is due partly to the bare grayish rocks of the treeless summits, but chiefly to atmospheric conditions." As plausible as this explanation might seem, Robert L. M. Underhill's 1958 article in *Appalachia*, the journal of the Appalachian Mountain Club, furnishes more than enough historical evidence to substantiate what has become known as the "snow theory." Noting that the rock theory most often has been based on poor information, Underhill quotes Reverend Jeremy

14

Belknap, one of the keenest observers of the White Mountains in the post-Revolutionary period:

> Should you ask what is the cause of the *white* appearance of these mountains, I would tell you in one word,—*snow*, which lies on them, commonly, from September or October till July. There is no white moss, nor white flint, nor white rocks, which can give any such reflection as is caused by the *snow*; and, after the snow is gone, they appear, at the distance of 60 or 70 miles, of a pale blue, inclining to a sky colour; at the distance of 10 or 15 miles, they are of the gray colour of the rock, inclining to brown.

With or without a gleaming coat of snow on their treeless peaks, the White Mountains remain a striking natural landmark as they loom above the horizon. Higher and more dramatic mountains there may be, but there are few others in the world whose craggy summits and forested glens have attracted as much attention.

Awe-inspiring U-shaped valleys were created by the movement of glaciers through the White Mountains. The cliffs of Cannon Mountain in Franconia Notch are shown here.

2. The People of Waumbekket Methna

For thousands of years before Europeans set foot on the North American continent, Algonquian-speaking peoples inhabited the eastern seaboard from the Canadian maritimes to the Carolina capes. Connected by a common language, as well as by similar cultural traditions and spiritual beliefs, these confederacies or tribes eventually developed distinct homelands within major river drainages up and down the Atlantic coast. Archaeological evidence reveals that during the long pre-contact period, countless generations of Native Americans lived their lives in harmony with a bountiful nature, employing new ideas when necessary to sustain their internal development and marking time by the changing seasons. Occupying the roles of hunters, gatherers, fishermen, and farmers, the original occupants of the East Coast established a unique realm that was forever changed by the European "discovery" of the New World.

The initial human penetration and settlement of what was to become the Algonquian northeast, including the territory encompassing the White Mountains, is estimated to have taken place about 10,700 years ago. It occurred after the retreat of the glaciers, but at the beginning of an abrupt climatic cold period that lasted for nearly a millennium. Identified by their fluted bifacial stone projectile points, the so-called "Palaeo-Indians" survived in a landscape of tundra and spruce woodlands by hunting large game, particularly caribou, as well as by making use of edible plants and small animals.

Evidence of these earliest inhabitants in the White Mountains has been found in several locations, most notably high up on the side of Mount Jasper in Berlin, where substantial outcroppings of rhyolite were mined and worked into flaked tools beginning about 7,000 years ago. Situated several hundred feet above the winding Androscoggin River in the shadow of the mighty Presidential Range, the Mount Jasper site features a quarry dug some 10 meters into solid ledge by members of a highly mobile population of Palaeo-Indians. Stopping only for brief periods to gather handfuls of easily-worked igneous rock, these ancient hunters removed an average of 80 pounds of rhyolite each year, manufacturing

Evidence of Palaeo-Indians in the Androscoggin valley exists in Berlin, New Hampshire, where a significant number of stone tools made from Mount Jasper rhyolite have been discovered.

it into such useful implements as knives, scrapers, drills, and spear points before departing on foot or by canoe for seasonal camps and hunting grounds. The discovery of a significant number of reworked projectile points that can be dated to just a few centuries before European settlement in the New World indicates the enduring significance of this site, which was recently listed in the *National Register of Historic Places*.

Archaeologists believe the Palaeo-Indian culture began to disappear around 5,000 years ago, a conclusion based partly on the predominance of projectile points dating from this time made of stone found in the Southeast and Midwest. During this transitional period, new migrations of people into northern New England clearly took place, with surviving artifacts reflecting a larger, denser population that depended for subsistence on the white-tailed deer, black bear, and elk, in addition to birds, freshwater fish, and shellfish. Climatic change and other influences brought about further modifications to Native American culture in the following centuries, including the introduction of seasonal crops, the creation of ceramic pottery, and the development of more sophisticated hunting patterns. These innovations transformed native lifestyles and established a dynamic culture that remained relatively intact until the age of European exploration and settlement.

The identity and demography of the Native American groups that inhabited the White Mountains in the centuries just before European contact is a complex matter whose full nature remains in shadow due to the original inhabitants' lack of a written language. As a consequence, modern-day scholars

These Abenaki "habitations and gardens" were recorded by Samuel de Champlain in the lower Saco River valley about 1605. Similar shelters were used in the White Mountains.

in search of a more multi-dimensional view of the region's native past have had to develop methodologies that ask new questions about a wide range of old sources, including archaeological evidence and oral tradition, as well as the culturally-biased reports made by sixteenth and seventeenth century European explorers, traders, and colonists. Reaching beyond the colorful accounts of "Indian wars," the recent re-examination of historic documents, previous scholarship, and modern archaeological data has yielded a more richly textured, if still incomplete, picture of Native American life during the pre-contact period.

There is general agreement today among archaeologists and anthropologists that the White Mountain region of Maine and New Hampshire was long the abode of the Abenaki, an eastern Algonquian sub-group whose homeland once stretched from the Iroquoian tribal lands in southern Quebec to the northern Massachusetts border, and from Passamaquoddy territory in eastern Maine to the shore of Lake Champlain in western Vermont. Translated to mean "people of the Dawnland" or "eastern people," the Abenaki (or Wabanaki) were composed of numerous bands of Native Americans historically identified by the names of the river valleys, or principal villages, in which they resided at the time of European contact. Among those groups dwelling in and around the White Mountains were the Pennacooks of the upper Merrimack and Pemigewasset Rivers, the Sokokis and Coosaukes of the upper Connecticut and Ammonoosuc watersheds, the Amarascoggin of the Androscoggin River, and the Pigwackets, who occupied the Saco River Valley and environs. Although the Winnipesaukees and Ossipees of the Lake Winnipesaukee region closely interacted with native people to the north, they spent a major part of their lives beyond the southern boundary of the White Mountains.

Data is lacking for a reliable estimate of early Abenaki populations in the White Mountains and vicinity, but it is reasonable to state that several thousand individuals inhabited the region in 1600, when New England as a whole probably supported a population of well over 100,000 native people. As recent scholarship has shown, these early inhabitants of the White Mountains were interrelated through marriage and communicated easily with each other in a Western Abenaki dialect. Such characteristics of Abenaki society seem to contradict the "riverine tribal model" long accepted by historians, suggesting it may not accurately reflect the political organization and migration patterns of closely-related Abenaki kinship groups inhabiting northern New England before the appearance of Europeans.

Abenaki life in the White Mountains previous to the first waves of European settlement revolved around seasonal encampments made up of loosely organized family bands. According to the late Gordon M. Day, an authority on the Western Abenaki:

> The villages of the Abenaki went through an annual cycle of migration—southward to seashore camps for the summer, northward to deep woods hunting camps in the fall and winter, returning to villages along the rivers for late fall feasting and spring fishing and planting.

As was true throughout northern New England, these small groups of linked families relied on hunting and fishing for their sustenance, and such was the abundance of food in field, forest, and stream that large reserves of dried meats, nuts, corn, smoked fish, and berries were placed in root cellars lined with bark each fall, in preparation for the lean winter months ahead. Abenaki villages, which were occupied only part of the year (causing one European to mistakenly observe

Several thousand Native Americans inhabited the mountain region in 1600. The first Abenaki to visit England made the voyage east about this time.

that their inhabitants were "naturally inclined to a roving and unsettled life"), were nearly always built alongside major waterways—the great water roads to the sea—and were "intertribal" to some degree. One of the largest such settlements in the White Mountains, "Pigwacket," was situated on a plateau above the Saco River intervales at present-day Fryeburg village, a short distance east of the border between Maine and New Hampshire. A series of well-worn trails (some dating back many thousands of years) connected this native community, containing some 200 inhabitants in 1642, with other Abenaki villages and seasonal campgrounds scattered throughout the mountains.

Abenaki society in the pre-contact period was patrilineal, with several related families living together in one long house covered in large sheets of bark. Fishing, hunting, warfare, and the construction of houses and canoes was the responsibility of the men, as was crafting hunting and war implements. Women and children shared such duties as cooking, cultivating crops (except tobacco), preparing skins and clothing, and gathering edible plants. Large groups of family bands were subject to the authority of a civil chief and a war chief, both of whom were selected for their outstanding abilities and could hold office for life or until bad behavior caused their removal from such positions of prestige and power. Important decisions were decided in council, where men, women, and young adults attended and where questions of importance were asked of the chief and presiding elders.

Like other Native American groups inhabiting New England, the Abenaki of the White Mountain region were great believers in the power of the spiritual

The Abenaki rarely ventured above the treeline on Mount Washington and other nearby peaks, believing these wind-swept areas to be the dwelling place of powerful spirits.

world and its influence over their natural environment. Moreover, during their long occupancy of this mountainous territory, the Abenaki developed a rich mythology that may have inspired the colorful, but highly inaccurate, stories told about Native Americans by the area's nineteenth century tavern and hotel keepers. One such fanciful tale, repeated by many White Mountain historians and purporting to give the Abenaki's version of the origin of Mount Washington, was first related in print by John H. Spaulding in his 1855 book, *Historical Relics of the White Mountains*:

> Cold storms were in the northern wilderness, and a lone red hunter wandered without food, chilled by the frozen wind. He lost his strength, and could find no game; and the dark cloud that covered his life-path made him weary of wandering. He fell down upon the snow, and a dream carried him to a wide, happy valley, filled with musical streams, where singing birds and game were plenty. His spirit cried aloud for joy; and the "*Great Master of Life*" waked him from his sleep, gave him a dry coal and a flint-pointed spear, telling him that by the shore of the lake he might live, and find fish with his spear, and fire from his dry coal. One night, when he had laid down his coal, and seen a warm fire spring up therefrom, with a blinding smoke, a loud voice came out of the flame, and a great noise, like thunder, filled the air; and there rose up a vast pile of broken rocks. Out of the cloud resting upon the top came numerous streams, dancing down, foaming cold; and the voice spake to the astonished red hunter, saying, "*Here the Great Spirit will dwell, and watch over his favorite children.*"

Under the direction of a shaman, who interpreted the spirit world and provided religious guidance to ordinary people, the Abenaki celebrated their connection to the natural world in stories passed down from one generation to the next. Among the tales handed down is one of *Bmola*, the dreaded "Wind Bird" or "Wind Eagle," which was said to generate strong winds from the summits of New England's high peaks. Legend has it that the mythical hero *Gluskab* captured the huge bird and bound its wings, but upon discovering that the air around the mountains became hot and heavy, he allowed the creature to return to its lofty perch to generate enough wind to cool his people and the forest animals.

As many historians have pointed out, the Abenaki seldom ventured above the timberline in the White Mountains, believing the barren, fog-enshrouded regions lying above the boreal forests to be the dwelling place of powerful spirits. This fear may have stemmed in part from the rumble of frequent landslides on the higher slopes of the mountains, a result of thin soils common to these upland locations. Certainly, the Abenaki's hesitancy to ascend Mount Washington is manifested by Governor John Winthrop's account of the first ascent of the mountain by a non-native in 1642: "Some of them accompanied

White Mts., N.H., Mts. Garfield and Lafayette and Ammonoosuc River.

Meaning "fish-place," the Ammonoosuc River was an important transportation route for the White Mountain Abenaki. Mounts Garfield and Lafayette tower in the distance.

him within 8 miles of the top, but durst go no further, telling him that no Indian ever dared go higher, and that he would die if he went."

Despite all the claims made in guidebooks and histories dating back to the 1830s, few authentic Abenaki place names for localities in the White Mountains seem to have survived. Indeed, it now seems clear many of the so-called Indian names associated with the region are more likely poor translations of the original spoken words or were bestowed by non-natives long after the contact period. For example, the naming of prominent natural features to venerate individuals was a concept alien to the native people, and yet such names as Passaconaway, Wonalancet, Chocorua, and Kancamagus now dot the landscape. All this is not to say that some ancient names have not survived, for a few such as "Ammonoosuc" (meaning "fish-place") and "Umbagog" (meaning "clear water" or "clear lake") have fortunately endured.

According to an 1806 letter written by Reverend Timothy Alden, the founder and president of Allegheny College and at one time Corresponding Secretary of the Massachusetts Historical Society, the Abenaki inhabiting the White Mountains used the term "Waumbekket Methna" when referring to higher peaks in the district. Samuel Adams Drake, a tireless nineteenth-century White Mountain promoter, thought this appellation for the "White Hills" bore evidence of genuineness, as it easily resolved itself into the Kennebec-Abenaki term "waubeghiket-amadinar," which translates to "white greatest mountains." But Drake also warned that the phrase, shortened to "Waumbek Methna" by many a nineteenth-century poet, might be merely a translation of the English "White Mountains." This is a caution some devotees of White Mountain place names have also applied to the term "Agiockochook," recorded in a 1736 captivity narrative as having been used by the Abenaki to denote the Presidential Range of mountains, as well as Mount Washington itself.

Many years before the original residents of the White Mountains opened their realm to European colonization, it was prophesied that a time would come when strangers would appear from the direction of the rising sun, putting an end to the happiness enjoyed by those who had dwelled for untold ages in the Dawnland. As if to corroborate this foreshadowing, a trickle of white explorers and settlers easing into northern New England in the early seventeenth century soon developed into a flood of land-hungry newcomers whose disdain for, and lack of understanding about, the Abenaki world generated what one student of this tumultuous period has called a "nightmare of competition, conflict, and chaos." Guarded by towering mountains whose storm-wracked peaks provided a unique sense of place from generation to generation, the native occupants of this powerful landscape were entering an age of turmoil and upheaval that would test their very survival as a people.

In 1884, Chief Joseph Laurent established a seasonal Abenaki camp in the Cathedral Woods in Intervale, New Hampshire. Members of his family continue the tradition today.

3. Exploring the Crystal Hills

The European quest for a northwest passage to "The Indies," as Japan, China, Indonesia, and India were collectively called by the thirteenth century, resulted in numerous sea voyages along the eastern coast of North America during the fifteenth and sixteenth centuries by a group of intrepid mariners. Among these adventurers were a handful who beheld the snow-capped crown of Mount Washington and its neighboring peaks as they journeyed along the rocky shores of Maine some 70 miles to the southeast—the closest proximity to these mountains one can attain when sailing on the Atlantic.

The name of the earliest seafarer to take notice of the White Mountains can never be known for certain, but historians generally give credit to the Florentine navigator Giovanni da Verrazano for being the first to record sighting them. In a letter to the King of France dated July 8, 1524, Verrazano set down his impressions of the country's interior as he observed it from the vicinity of Casco Bay: "We departed, skirting the coast between east and north, which we found very beautiful, open and bare of forests, with high mountains back inland, growing smaller toward the shore of the sea." Later explorers, in their own search for a direct route to the East, discovered instead a land of seemingly endless bounty whose backdrop was an isolated mountain range conspicuous for its height. Of course, European mapmakers were anxious to render both the topography and toponymy of eastern New England based on these observations, and thus several contemporary maps of the region, including Gerardus Mercator's 1569 "Mappemonde," vaguely acknowledge the existence of the White Mountain segment of the Appalachian chain. These less-than-realistic delineations may seem primitive by today's standards, but it did not prevent seafarers of 400 years' past from utilizing them to navigate the relatively unknown waters off the New England coastline.

As the seventeenth century began, Europeans were in regular contact with Native Americans traveling seasonally between the coast and the White Mountains, and by 1605 several Abenaki had made the return journey to England, where their appearance caused a sensation. Having established

The White Mountains served as a navigational device for explorers. This 1799 map notes, "The White Hills appear many leagues off at sea like white clouds just rising above the horizon."

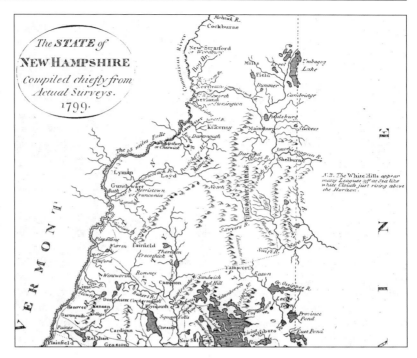

peaceful relations with the native inhabitants of the Penobscot River the previous fall, French explorer Samuel de Champlain voyaged along the Maine coast in July of 1605, noting as he passed the entrance to Portland Harbor, "From here large mountains are seen to the west, in which is the dwelling place of a savage captain called Aneda, who encamps near the river Quinibequy [Kennebec]." Two decades later, the Englishman Christopher Levett, the pioneer colonist of Casco Bay, made what was probably the first reference in print specifically to Mount Washington in his account of a voyage to New England in 1623 and 1624:

> This River [presumably the Saco], as I am told by the *Salvages*, commeth from a great mountain called the Christall hill, being as they say 100 miles in the Country, yet it is to be seene at the sea side, and there is no ship arives in *New England*, either to the West so farre as *Cape Cod*, or to the East so farre as *Monhiggen*, but they see this mountain the first land, if the weather be cleere.

Curiosity about the exact nature of the "Christall hill" may have invoked images of crystals and precious gems sparkling in the sunlight, but it was the ongoing rivalry among Dutch, English, and French interests over control of this part of the New World that first caused Europeans to wonder about the valuable resources surely laying hidden in the mythical landscape to the north. History has shown that even before permanent settlements along the coast were firmly established, friction over the right to trade for beaver skins and catch fish in offshore grounds long used by sailors from western England initiated a struggle for supremacy that would last for the next century and a half. The Abenaki of northern New England, caught in the middle, soon realized resistance to the ever-growing wave of European immigration was futile.

In an effort to establish a lasting hold on lands between the present Hudson and Saint Lawrence Rivers, numerous government officials and courtiers in 1620 had persuaded England's King James to create the Council for New England, with authority to grant "patents" and encourage trade throughout the disputed territory. Plagued during its brief existence by poor management and political maneuvering, the council in the 1620s granted vast tracts of land between the Merrimack and Kennebec Rivers to John Mason and Sir Ferdinando Gorges, two of London's strongest advocates for development of New England as a royal colony. Focusing his attention on the Piscataqua River and its many tributaries, Mason christened his patent "New Hampshire," after his native county in England. Like Gorges, who held title to much of what is now southern Maine, Mason served as an absentee landlord over a region of scattered fishing outposts he hoped would evolve rapidly into thriving coastal communities mirroring those in England. When he died in 1635, however, Mason left a cluster of settlements struggling for existence in a sometimes harsh and always challenging

In 1631, the Laconia Company authorized Captain Walter Neale to lead an exploration party into the White Mountains. Mount Carrigain's peak (left) dominates the Pemigewasset Wilderness.

environment, where boundary disputes over lands granted by the rival Massachusetts Bay Colony seemed to be the rule rather than the exception.

An important consequence of the Mason and Gorges grants was the founding of a financial partnership known as the Laconia Company. Responsible for surveying the territory north to the "River of Canada" (Saint Lawrence), in which a fabulous source of fish and furs known as the "Lake of the Iroquois" was presumably located, the Laconia Company in 1631 authorized one of its directors, Captain Walter Neale, to lead an exploration party deep into the interior. Indications are that this group of Englishmen approached or even investigated the "Crystal Hills," and in his 1812 *History of New Hampshire* Jeremy Belknap went so far as to state, "In the course of their travels, they visited the White Mountains, which they described . . . to be a ridge, extending an hundred leagues." Because his chronicle was based on sources published many years after Neale's undertaking, and no first-hand account of the trip has survived, we can only speculate on the route taken by this daring band of trailblazers. What does seem certain is that information brought back by Neale and his companions concerning the wondrous land beyond the coast fired the imagination of at least one newly-arrived settler in the "Plantation of Pascataway" by the name of Darby Field.

Born in Boston, England, about 1610, Field voyaged to New England around 1636, supposedly to escape religious persecution. By 1638 he had settled near the Squamscott River in Exeter, the third town organized in the state. Credited with being the first European to visit and explore the White Mountains, as well as the first to ascend Mount Washington, Field made two expeditions into the region in 1642, just a decade after Walter Neale's assault on the wilderness and only 22 years after the landing in Plymouth by the Pilgrims.

The evidence for Darby Field's accomplishments, which are remarkable in the history of mountaineering in both America and Europe for their early date, is irrefutable, owing to a recently uncovered letter written on June 29, 1642, just a few weeks after Field's pioneering climb. Composed by Thomas Gorges, who was then serving as deputy governor of the Province of Maine on behalf of his cousin, Sir Ferdinando Gorges, the letter describes Field's journey up the Saco River to the White Mountains and supplies important clues as to the route taken to the summit of Mount Washington. The most important passage in Gorges's letter reads:

> . . . you desier a relation of the white hills. This much I certify of accordinge as it was sent to me by him that discovered them whose name was Darby Feild [sic] of pascataqua who about a month since with some 3 or 4 Indians undertook the voyage, went first to Pigwackett, a place on the Saco river accordinge to my draught now 23 leagues from Mr Vines his house, hence he travailled some 80 miles as he sayeth & came to a mountain, went over it, & a 2d & a 3d, at length came to a ledge of rocks which he conceaved to be 12 miles high, very steep, uppon which he travailed going to a rocke that was at the end of that which he judged 2 miles high, very steep, yet he

adventured up, but one Indian accompaynge him, the most being fearfull. At the top it was not above 20 foot square, wher he sate with much fear some 5 hours time the clouds passing under him makinge a terrible noyse against the mountains. Thence he discovered some 80 miles farther a very glorious white mountain & between 2 other great mountains as he judged some 100 miles . . . a mighty river bearing North & by East from him of which like or sea he could see noe end. On this mountain, he mett with terrible freesing weather and, as I took it, on the top of the ledge or rocke & at the foot of them were 2 litle ponds, 1 of a curious red colour, the other black. The [latter] dyed his handkerchief very blacke, the former did not alter the collours. Ther wer many rattle snakes but he receaved noe harm. He intends as I hear for them a 2d voyage . . . about a fortnight hence. I intend with Mr V[ines] & Mr Joc[elyn] for Pasc[ataqua] & to take an ampler account. Our resolution hold for the voyage as yet about the end of August.

Prior to the discovery of the Gorges letter, the only known account of Field's arduous trip into the White Mountains was found in the journal of Governor John Winthrop of Massachusetts. Being the earlier of the two, the Gorges rendition is probably more reliable, apart from Field's wildly exaggerated distances. Gorges's description also differs significantly from Winthrop's by mentioning three preliminary peaks over which Field and his party ventured before passing "2 litle ponds" (presumably the Lakes of the Clouds) and scaling Mount Washington's summit cone. This information does not fit with the long-held belief that Field approached Mount Washington from the east, utilizing the Ellis River Valley and Boott Spur, the mountain's southeast shoulder, to attain the area above the treeline. Rather, a more westerly route traversing the "southern Presidentials," a great ridge extending for some 8 miles southwest of Mount Washington's summit, is now suggested.

If Darby Field's exact route through *terra incognita* to the top of Mount Washington remains problematic, the motivation behind his perilous adventure seems more obvious, especially if it is remembered that he was part of an English middle class accustomed to "remarkable providences" and fascinated by myths, legends, tall tales, and treasure hunting, particularly as they related to the New World. This preoccupation with hidden riches is made obvious in a letter written by Thomas Gorges in September 1641: "In this country there are latly found very rare stones . . . with all the squares poynted as if by the hand of an expert worker." Governor John Winthrop's journal, which notes Darby Field's second visit to Mount Washington, attests to his interest in discovering fabulous gemstones atop the Northeast's highest peak:

> He found there much Muscovy glass [mica], they could rive out pieces
> of 40 feet long and 7 or 8 broad. When he came back to the Indians, he

Darby Field was the first European to climb 6,288-foot Mount Washington. His 1642 route probably took him across the Southern Presidentials, shown here.

found them drying themselves by the fire, for they had had a great tempest of wind and rain. About a month after he went again, with five or six of his company, then they had some wind on the top, and some clouds above them which hid the sun. They brought some stones which they supposed had been diamonds, but they were most crystal.

Eager to see the White Mountains for himself, Thomas Gorges made the difficult journey north around the end of August 1642, as he had planned, for in a letter dated September 24, 1642, he states, "I have bin at the White Hills." Accompanied by Councillor of the Province of Maine Richard Vines, Esquire, and "divers others," Gorges made the trip in 15 days, a fact noted by Governor Winthrop in the only surviving narrative of the journey. "They went up Saco river in birch canoes, and that way, they found it 90 miles to Pegwagget, an Indian town, but by land it is but 60," wrote Winthrop. Gorges's party observed thousands of acres of rich meadow land on their upriver journey, which required portaging around ten waterfalls. From the Abenaki village in present-day Fryeburg, Maine, they "went up hill (for the most part), about 30 miles in woody lands, then they went about 7 or 8 miles upon shattered rocks, without tree or grass, very steep all the way." Winthrop's highly accurate description of the above-treeline zone of the Presidential Range must have come directly from Gorges, for he continues, "At the top is a plain about three or four miles over, all shattered stones, and upon that is another rock or spire, about a mile in height, and about an acre of ground at the top." Closely examining the upper plateau on Mount Washington, Gorges's team felt sure they had discovered the source of four of the great rivers of the region—the Connecticut, Saco, Androscoggin, and Kennebec—"each of them so much water, at the first issue, as would drive a mill." Tributaries for all, except the Kennebec, do arise from the shoulders of this great mountain, so perhaps this geographic *faux pas* can be excused. Recognizing the Presidential Range as part of a larger chain of mountains, Gorges's company surmised that "the mountain runs E. and W. 30 or 40 miles, but the peak is above all the rest." Commenting on their search for Darby Field's "shining stones," Winthrop observed, "They found nothing worth their pains."

The search for priceless minerals atop the Crystal Hills seems to have ended as quickly as it began, with interest in the White Mountains fading away after these few daring exploits in 1642. Not until 1725 do we find credible documentation of another "ranging party" making its way through the silent forests and up Mount Washington's craggy slopes. Yet, during this 80-year interval the majestic hills were not forgotten, for in 1672 an interesting description of the region appeared in *New-Englands Rarities Discovered*, a book by the traveler and writer John Josselyn. An accomplished scientist and an independent observer of "the wonders of a paradise he envisioned in New England," Josselyn visited the Province of Maine from 1638 to 1639 and again from 1663 to 1671. In his book, which was followed two years later by *An Account of Two Voyages to New-England*, we see the first appearance in print of the term "White Mountains:"

> Fourscore miles (upon a direct line) to the Northwest of *Scarborow*, a Ridge of Mountains run Northwest and Northeast an hundred

Darby Field's account of precious stones atop Mount Washington encouraged others to explore the White Mountains. These "priceless minerals" turned out to be quartz crystals and mica.

Leagues, known by the name of the *White Mountains*, upon which lieth Snow all the year, and is a Land-mark twenty miles off at Sea. It is rising ground from the Sea shore to these Hills, and they are inaccessible but by the Gullies which the dissolved Snow hath made; in these Gullies grow *Saven* Bushes, which being taken hold of are a good help to the climbing Discoverer; upon the top of the highest of these Mountains is a large Level or Plain of a days journey over, whereon nothing grows but Moss; at the farther end of this Plain is another Hill called the *Sugar-loaf*, to outward appearance a rude heap of massie stones piled one upon another, and you may as you ascend step from one stone to another, as if you were going up a pair of stairs, but winding still about the Hill till you come to the top, which will require half a days time, and yet it is not above a Mile, where there is also a Level of about an Acre of ground, with a pond of clear water in the midst of it, which you may hear run down, but how it ascends is a mystery. From this rocky Hill you may see the whole Country round about; it is far above the lower Clouds, and from hence we beheld a Vapour (like a great Pillar) drawn up by the Sun Beams out of a great Lake or Pond into the Air, where it was formed into a Cloud. The Country beyond these Hills Northward is daunting terrible, being full of rocky Hills, as thick as Mole-hills in a Meadow, and cloathed with infinite thick Woods.

John Josselyn's 1672 chronicle resonates with personal knowledge of the White Mountains, but we cannot be sure of the sources for his quaint and curious description. In *An Account of Two Voyages*, published in 1674, Josselyn anticipates future interest in the district's timber and agricultural potential when he writes, "Between the mountains are many ample rich and pregnant valleys as ever eye beheld, beset on each side with variety of goodly Trees, the grass man-high unmowed, uneaten and uselesly withering." Perhaps as a reaction to criticism to his first book, his second corrects his previous statement about snow lying on the mountains year-round by excepting the month of August.

The year 1677 saw the publication of William Hubbard's history of King Philip's War, a work summarizing that brief (1675–1676) but bloody conflict between Native Americans and English colonists in southern New England. Led by the Wampanoag chief Metacomet (called "King Philip" by the English), groups of Native Americans from southern and central New England, along with bands of Abenaki from the north, attacked English settlements, wreaking havoc and causing Puritan New England to question whether the "infinite thick woods" between the coast and the White Mountains would ever be safe again. Entitled *The Present State of New-England. Being a Narrative of the Troubles with the Indians in New England*, Hubbard's history contained a map of New England showing two hillocks north of Lake Winnipesaukee labeled as "The White Hills,"

Passaconaway was a legendary Pennacook sachem who tried to maintain peace with the early settlers of the Merrimack valley. A mountain in the Sandwich Range bears his name.

the first time the White Mountains were specifically located on a map. Based on a woodcut by John Foster, this now-famous map was designed to illustrate the extent of English settlement in the region by including many of the communities attacked and destroyed during this violent encounter. Curiously, this map appeared in the London edition of Hubbard's history with the words "Wine Hills" inserted, an obvious misread on the part of the wood engraver copying Foster's original.

King Philip's War marked a turning point in seventeenth century encounters between Europeans and Native Americans, but it was far from the worst disaster to occur during that lengthy period of tension and upheaval in New England. That honor goes to the "Great Dying," a cataclysmic scourge brought upon the native population by epidemics of smallpox, measles, typhus, and other afflictions from which they had no immunity. Spreading into the White Mountain region from the mouth of the Saco in 1617 and up the Connecticut River (on the western fringe of the mountains) by 1635, these contagious diseases greatly reduced native populations, perhaps by as much as 90 percent.

By the middle of the seventeenth century, an attitude of friendly curiosity had turned to distrust and hostility as the native population of northern New England watched their numbers rapidly dwindle and their intertribal relationships disintegrate, the latter mostly due to a burgeoning fur trade and the introduction of firearms. The demand for furs strained the native economy by using up time previously spent in search of large game for food and skins; it also made natives much more aware of the importance of territorial boundaries, a concept foreign to the Abenaki before European notions of private land use and ownership were imposed on the region. The intermingling of cultures was further strained by the effects of the liquor trade, a significant component in English and French efforts to maintain Abenaki allegiances as the century wore on. All of these factors combined in the 1670s to bring about King Philip's War, a battle that inaugurated a century of discord and bloodshed throughout much of New England.

Just as whole native villages vanished like wisps of smoke during the great plague, so too have all but a few of the names of the original inhabitants who resided in and around the White Mountains during this turbulent era. Remembered in a graceful 4,000-foot peak in the Sandwich Range of the southern White Mountains, Passaconaway was a legendary Pennacook sachem who was present when the Pilgrims landed and who, in 1629, granted a considerable tract of land between the Piscataqua and Merrimack Rivers to the Reverend John Wheelwright and others of the Massachusetts Bay Colony. Displaying a character of a remarkably high order, Passaconaway early on established a policy of peace with the English, restraining his followers from participating in the "Indian wars" even when provoked by obvious English treachery and deceit. About 1669, weary with the burden of years, Passaconaway abdicated his chieftainship to his son Wonalancet, "a sober and grave person . . . always loving and friendly to the English." An old tradition has it that at his death Passaconaway was carried to Mount Washington in a sleigh drawn by wolves, whence he rose toward Heaven in a chariot of fire.

Like his father, Wonalancet desired peace, but thought it best to retreat with his people for a time to the protection of the White Mountains and the Connecticut River intervales to the north. Many of the Pennacooks eventually returned to their homeland, but deception and poor treatment by colonists took their toll until a time came for the Pennacooks to "cross out their account." Disheartened, Wonalancet removed to the French mission village at St. Francis, in southern Quebec, where he may have died sometime around 1697.

Kancamagus, the grandson of Passaconaway by Nanamocomuck (his eldest son), became sachem of the Pennacooks around 1685. According to historian Frederick W. Kilbourne, "This resolute warrior made several attempts to retain the friendship of the colonists, but was unsuccessful and finally yielded, after many slights and much-ill treatment, to the warlike and patriotic party in the confederation." In 1689, accompanied by Saco River Abenaki, he led an attack on Dover, but after his wife and children were captured by the English in 1690, Kancamagus signed a peace treaty at Sagadahoc. It seems likely that Kancamagus followed in his uncle's footsteps, retreating to St. Francis after this time, the peace-loving members of his tribe having dispersed throughout the Merrimack and its feeder streams. Today, his name is preserved in a modest White Mountain peak northeast of Waterville Valley, as well as in a scenic highway traversing the White Mountain National Forest between the towns of Lincoln and Conway.

Increasing tensions between the English and French and their native allies during Queen Anne's War (1703–1713) and Dummer's War (1721–1726) brought the White Mountains to the forefront as a region of strategic importance. Scouting parties of Massachusetts and New Hampshire militia units frequently ventured into the Ammonoosuc, Pemigewasset, Swift, Saco, and Androscoggin Valleys searching for the tracks of war parties, hoping to rescue captives and obtain native scalps for which generous bounties were being offered. One such expedition, headed by Lieutenant Thomas Baker of Northampton, Massachusetts, and containing about 30 men, confronted a group of Abenaki at present-day Plymouth, mortally wounding their chief, Waternomee. On another patrol in April 1725, according to the Reverend Jeremy Belknap, a group of rangers ascended Mount Washington, where they "found the snow four feet deep on the northwest side, the summit almost bare of snow though covered with white frost and ice, and the alpine pond frozen." Since there was no reason to believe the local Abenaki had withdrawn to the mountaintop, this expedition, the last to the top of Mount Washington until the year 1774, was probably undertaken out of pure curiosity.

Throughout this time of general unrest in the White Mountains, the Abenaki community of Pigwacket continued to draw the attention of ranging parties. Such was the situation in 1704, when a large company of Massachusetts soldiers led by Major Winthrop Hilton invaded the "Pequawket country," but found the village's 100 wigwams and stockade fort deserted. In the past, it had been easy for members of the Pigwacket tribe to slip away silently into the forest in response to threats, but now that the ancient village was only a two days' march from English settlements, more drastic measures were required. Having received word of the impending attack by Hilton and his men, many Pigwackets had withdrawn north to the St. Francis village, where they remained with their chief, Atecuando (also known as Squando), until the close of Queen Anne's War in 1713. Two decades later, in the wake of renewed hostilities, Pigwacket became the scene of one of the most widely known military events in colonial New England history: the "Battle of Lovewell's Pond." Thirty-four scalp hunters, led by the daring Captain John Lovewell, made their way from what is now Nashua, to Ossipee Pond and thence to Saco (now Lovewell's) Pond, not far from Pigwacket. On May 8, 1725, two days after their arrival, Lovewell's men engaged some 40 Abenaki led by the Pigwacket chief Paugus. The ensuing struggle resulted in heavy casualties, including Lovewell and 19 of his compatriots, as well as Paugus and an equal number of his followers. A major result of this legendary skirmish was a general shift in the Abenaki population in the White Mountains to the north and east, away from entanglements of the English-French rivalry.

This pivotal event at modern-day Fryeburg notwithstanding, numbers of Pigwackets returned to the upper Saco Valley soon after the Lovewell battle, where they reoccupied their old hunting grounds seasonally for several more decades. When the Maine/New Hampshire border was being surveyed in 1741, a work party came upon an encampment of Abenaki near Pigwacket and, intimidated by their many questions, turned back. Among those in this group may have been the legendary Chocorua, whose name would be connected to the

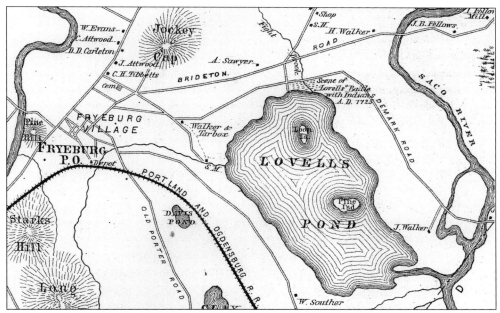

In 1725, a group of Massachusetts soldiers attacked the Pigwacket Indians in present-day Fryeburg, Maine. The site of "Lovell's Battle" is indicated on this 1880 map.

Chocorua was an Abenaki well known to early settlers. His death is depicted in an engraving from a painting by the artist Thomas Cole.

second-most famous peak in the White Mountains by 1790. The following story about Chocorua originally appeared in the first edition (1876) of M.F. Sweetser's *The White Mountains: A Handbook for Travellers*, and no doubt contains a smattering of truth interspersed with a liberal dose of hyperbole. By tradition, credit for preserving this tale is usually given to Jonathan Gilman, an early resident of the town of Tamworth, which lies in Mount Chocorua's shadow.

> When the Pequawket Indians retreated to Canada, after Lovewell's battle, Chocorua refused to leave the ancient home of his people and the graves of his forefathers. He remained behind, and was friendly to the in-coming white settlers, and especially with one Campbell, who lived near what is now Tamworth. He had a son, in whom all his hopes and love were centred. On one occasion he was obliged to go to Canada to consult with his people at St. Francis, and, wishing to spare his son the labors of the long journey, he left him with Campbell until his return. The boy was welcomed to the hut of the pioneer, and tenderly cared for. One day, however, he found a small bottle of poison, which had been prepared for a mischievous fox, and, with the unsuspecting curiosity of the Indians, he drank a portion of it. Chocorua returned only to find his boy dead and buried. The improbable story of his fatality failed to satisfy the heart-broken chief, and his spirit demanded vengeance. Campbell went home from the fields one day, and saw the dead and mangled bodies of his wife and

children on the floor of the hut. He tracked Chocorua and found him on the crest of the mountain, and shot him down, while the dying Indian invoked curses on the white men.

Another version of the Chocorua story seems to contain more of the ring of truth to it, asserting that he:

> was a blameless and inoffensive Indian, a friend of the whites, but, during one of the Massachusetts campaigns against the red men, when the Province gave a bounty of 100 pounds for every scalp brought into Boston, a party of hunters pursued the unresisting chieftain and shot him on this mountain, in order to get the bounty-money.

Regardless of the manner in which Chocorua met his demise, his legend, coupled with images of the solemn peak bearing his name, supplied fodder for many nineteenth century writers—including Longfellow—who sought to honor this "noble savage" in their literary efforts. One of the earliest of these works was composed by Mrs. Lydia Maria Child for the 1830 edition of *The Token*, an annual published in Boston. Entitled "Chocorua's Curse," the piece concludes with the wounded chief uttering the following words as he passed from this life to the next:

> A curse upon ye, white men! May the Great Spirit curse ye when he speaks in the clouds, and his words are fire! Chocorua had a son—and ye killed him while the sky looked bright! Lightning blast your crops! Wind and fire destroy your dwellings! The Evil Spirit breathe death upon your cattle! Your graves lie in the war path of the Indian! Panthers howl, and wolves fatten over your bones! Chocorua goes to the Great Spirit—his curse stays with the white man!

Many years after Chocorua's death, local tavern keepers and hoteliers continued to promote his curse as genuine, even though towns in the vicinity of the famous mountain were never subjected to Indian raids, pestilence, or other calamities.

The outbreak of yet another Anglo-French conflict in Europe in 1744, known as King George's War in the colonies, touched off further incidents of violence in and around the White Mountain region over the next few years. By the Treaty of Falmouth in 1749, a peace agreement was reached, but its effects proved only tentative, as the general frontier struggle known as the French and Indian War erupted in 1754. This decisive confrontation witnessed an attack on the St. Francis village by a detachment of Rogers' Rangers in October 1759. Legend has it that one group of these Massachusetts men, carrying off the church plate, candlesticks, and a large silver image, attempted to return home through the White Mountains, but became disoriented and everyone perished from starvation except one. The candlesticks, so the story goes, were located near Lake Memphremagog in 1816, but the silver image was never discovered.

The defeat of French Canada by the British in 1760, and the resulting Treaty of Paris in 1763, brought a period of peace to the northern frontier that allowed for the creation of permanent English settlements throughout the White Mountains of New Hampshire and Maine. The burgeoning colonial population, poised on the southern fringe of the mountains, now entered the region unfettered by threats from the north or the relatively small number of Abenaki remaining in the area. A new era in the history of the White Mountain wilderness was just beginning.

Mount Chocorua, at the eastern end of the Sandwich Range, is the second-most famous peak in the White Mountains, and one of the most photographed in the world.

4. SETTLERS AND SCIENTISTS

The colonial settlement of the White Mountain region followed an arrangement common to many areas of northern New England in the years just before the American Revolution. Unlike in earlier times, when provincial governments granted townships to settlers who also acted as "proprietors," owning home lots clustered in villages and holding pasture land and woodlots in common with other shareholders, many of the earliest towns in the White Mountains were granted to people of influence who had no interest in relocating to the North Country. These absentee landlords, some of whom received their grants as payment for military service during the French and Indian wars, immediately hired surveyors to create town plans divided into a grid pattern of roughly 50-acre parcels that did not allow for a centralized village and that virtually ignored the local topography. The desire for profit, rather than concern for the quality of life in the developing townships, was the main objective of these often wealthy landholders.

During the early 1760s, a handful of hardy pioneers, anxious to take advantage of the agricultural, forest, and mineral wealth of this newly-opened territory, purchased farmsteads from the proprietors (or were given land in an effort to meet certain grant stipulations) and journeyed to the White Mountains. They established several "gateway" towns, including Fryeburg, Maine; and Conway, Plymouth, Warren, Campton, Sandwich, Albany, Tamworth, and Lancaster in New Hampshire. The earliest settlers of the latter town, hailing mostly from western Massachusetts, were astonished to encounter the "Upper Cohos Meadows," vast tracts of fertile intervale lying alongside the Connecticut River. And yet they faced many challenges. Commenting on their efforts to establish a foothold at the northern edge of the mountains, the Reverend A.N. Somers, author of the *History of Lancaster, New Hampshire* (1899), wrote:

> Knowing that great hardships were in waiting for them through a long winter, they gave themselves resolutely to the task of wresting a living from the forests. They managed, however, to subsist on game together with such roots and berries as they found palatable. One can

scarcely imagine a company of people going into one of our long winters, more than fifty miles from the nearest settlement, without the semblance of food in their cabins, and forced to rely upon the flesh of wild animals from day to day for subsistence.

Fortunately for the settlers that winter [1764–1765], this region abounded in moose, and other game and fur-bearing animals. Then the streams abounded in fish of the best quality, easily taken in the spring. The Connecticut river then teemed with salmon every spring, and the settlers soon came to look to it as a source of supply in meat. The fine flavor of the salmon must have afforded them a pleasant change from moose and bear meat to which they would be confined for the greater part of the year.

We must not forget, however, that David Page brought with him in April, twenty head of stock, and during the summer added twenty more. They must have had milk in abundance; and in case of necessity could have dressed and eaten their cattle. The only wonder is, how they subsisted so long on a flesh diet without bread or vegetables. They were probably but little worse off than other settlers in the nearest settlements. Their cattle wintered well and everything assumed a promising aspect in the spring of 1765. They planted again, but reaped a scanty harvest, that, and the succeeding year; but the next year, their fourth year of effort was crowned by a most abundant

Fryeburg, Maine; and Conway, New Hampshire, are the oldest towns in the White Mountains. Their earliest residents struggled to survive in a harsh environment.

harvest. As soon as the people learned to raise a variety of crops, and not trust their all upon a single one, the period of want and uncertainty was passed.

Within a few years of the opening of these new townships, the pace of land granting quickened, so that before the outbreak of the Revolution, most of the towns existing today in the White Mountain region had been laid out and mapped, although some had yet to see land cleared for farmsteads. Among this second group were the present day New Hampshire communities of Jefferson, Littleton, Franconia, Berlin, Whitefield, Bartlett, Bethlehem, Lisbon, Randolph, Carroll, Thornton, Woodstock, and Shelburne (which then included Gorham). Just over the state boundary into Maine, efforts were underway to found the mountainous townships of Gilead, Lovell, Stow, and Bethel.

Mimicking the habits of the Native Americans who long occupied these mountains, the early white settlers made their way into the region by canoe or on foot over ancient trails in summer, and on snowshoes through the woods or on the ice of frozen rivers in winter. During the coldest season, their most frequent visitors were the Abenaki, who clung to their old hunting grounds and repeatedly expressed a legal claim to the territory. The settlers bartered for wild meat, tallow, and fur in exchange for corn and sugar. "They seemed to be in a measure exiled from the world," wrote the nineteenth-century historian Dr. Nathaniel Tuckerman True of the nascent communities on the upper Androscoggin. "Luxuries were unknown; but they had stout hearts, and the earth, as soon as the trees were felled and burned, yielded most bountiful crops." In response to their isolated condition, settlers began constructing crude roads to connect their fledgling communities with seaports to the south and southeast.

According to Lucy Crawford's *History of the White Mountains, from the First Settlement of Upper Coos and Pequaket* (1846), the first book devoted solely to this region, one such route of great importance was opened through the "Notch of the White Mountains" (Crawford Notch) in response to a discovery made in 1771 by two hunters, Timothy Nash and Benjamin Sawyer. In her account, which differs from later versions that credit Nash alone, the men were part of a larger group of newly-arrived settlers in "Coos and also in Essex, Vermont" who were searching for "a passage through the White Mountains . . . where a road could be made so as to reach the easterly part of the state and the coast of Maine." One day, while on Cherry Mountain in Jefferson, the two men supposedly noticed a rift in the mountains to the southwest some 8 miles away, and Nash "climbed a tree to be sure of the fact." Steering for the opening, they came upon the headwaters of the Saco River and followed it with some difficulty through the narrow gorge, eventually making their way to Portsmouth where they told Governor Benning Wentworth of the discovery. Realizing the benefits that would come from a direct trade route between the upper

Connecticut Valley and the lower settlements, Wentworth promised to grant a large tract north of the notch if Nash and Sawyer could bring a horse safely from Jefferson to Portsmouth. With much exertion, they accomplished this difficult feat, which required lowering the horse over several projecting cliffs. Legend has it that Sawyer, after maneuvering the poor animal over a large obstruction beyond the southern end of the notch, drank the last drop from his rum bottle, and breaking it upon the ledge, christened it Sawyer's Rock. This familiar landmark can still be seen today on the western side of Route 302, some 3 miles north of Bartlett village.

Governor Wentworth made good on his promise in 1773, granting what became known as "Nash and Sawyer's Location" to the two men on condition that they should make a good road through their tract and settle at least five families on it within five years. Although Nash and Sawyer seem to have squandered the proceeds of their grant, which included land running north from

The famous "Gate of the Notch" was supposedly discovered in 1771 by hunters Timothy Nash and Benjamin Sawyer. The headwaters of the Saco River flow through this narrow defile at the north end of Crawford Notch.

the "Gate of the Notch" to a line west of Bretton Woods, construction of the road through the notch was begun in the mid-1770s. The first merchandise carried down from Lancaster to the coast was a barrel of tobacco, and the first commodity brought back was a barrel of rum, whose contents, it was said, were mostly consumed on the way back "through the politeness of those who helped to manage the affair." Improved greatly in 1785, the first road through Crawford Notch was:

> a singular specimen of highway engineering, being laid out, in the main, fifty or sixty feet higher than the later turnpike, being so steep in places that it was necessary to draw horses and wagons up with ropes, and crossing the Saco no less than thirty-two times in ascending the valley.

It is worth noting that sections of this rugged thoroughfare doubtless followed the course of an old Abenaki trail through which English captives were led to Canada as early as 1746, when a raiding party attacked Gorham, Maine, and returned north through the notch.

In 1774, about the time work was beginning on a road through Crawford Notch, the Province of New Hampshire hired John Evans of Fryeburg to head up a work team to construct a road between Conway and Shelburne through the "Eastern Pass," a broad valley on the east side of Mount Washington where the waters of the Peabody and Ellis Rivers start their courses north and south, respectively. Winding around ledges and through thickly forested glens, this wilderness road provided townships north of the Presidential Range with another important link to the outside world. The Eastern Pass would later be named Pinkham Notch for Daniel Pinkham, a son of Captain Joseph Pinkham, who in 1790 moved with his family from Madbury to Jackson, a township "opened up" in 1778 at the southern entrance to the valley.

The emigration of people into the White Mountains from the south was slowed but not halted by the Revolutionary War. Far removed from the panic and confusion in New England's older communities, the impoverished backwoods settlements were relatively safe havens from British reprisals. While coastal towns worried about bombardment from English naval forces, farmers in the hill country were busy clearing land, burning trees to make potash, and erecting water-powered saw and grist mills. The slowly-evolving frontier hamlets in the White Mountain region were not immune from attack, however. Soon after the war began, the early Jefferson settler Colonel Joseph Whipple was made a prisoner in his house by a party of Abenaki "under the control of the English." Permitted by his captors to go to his bedroom to secure some clothes for his journey north, Whipple escaped through a window, went to a field where his men were at work, and ordered each of them to shoulder a fence stake as he would a gun. Seeing what they thought were a group of armed men approaching the house, the natives fled the area.

Rock-strewn and unnavigable, many rivers and streams in the White Mountains nevertheless furnished water power for saw and grist mills used by early white settlers.

Perhaps the most thrilling event to occur in the White Mountains during the Revolution was the now-famous "Last Indian Raid in New England," which occurred in the upper Androscoggin Valley on August 2 and 3, 1781. Led by Tomhegan (also "Tumkin Hagen"), a small band of Abenaki "painted and armed with guns, tomahawks and scalping knives" plundered several houses in Newry, Bethel, and Gilead, Maine, capturing three men and killing a fourth in the latter township. Marching west into New Hampshire, the attackers then raided several cabins in Shelburne, capturing an African-American man named Plato and killing Peter Poor, an early settler. As a result of this assault, a number of families left the area, and a party of 30 men were sent north from Fryeburg through the Cold River Valley and Evans Notch in a futile attempt to pursue Tomhegan and the others toward Canada. Shelburne's inhabitants, the night of the attack, are said to have spent many sleepless hours listening to the "whoops and cries of the Indians" from atop a rocky prominence still referred to as "Hark Hill."

Unlike Tomhegan, who had long resented white settlement in the upper Androscoggin Valley, many of the Native Americans who were well-known to residents of the oldest White Mountain towns sympathized with the American cause during the Revolution. Among the names that have come down to us are Captain Philips, Sabattis, Captain Swassin, Peol, Matalloch, and Molly Ockett.

Born around 1740 at Saco, Maine, Molly Ockett was a Pigwacket who spent most of her long life among old families of the White Mountains. Her skills as a healer, story-teller, and craftswoman were legendary. It has been suggested that it was Molly Ockett who taught the curative powers of various roots and herbs to "Granny Stalbird," a servant of Colonel Whipple of Jefferson who became a noted "doctress" in the region in the late eighteenth and early nineteenth centuries. Credited with saving the life of Hannibal Hamlin, Lincoln's first vice-president, when he was an infant, Molly Ockett died at Andover, Maine, in 1816.

The early history of the White Mountains is replete with many tales of adventure and misfortune, dramatic evidence of a landscape that was viewed as both fascinating and forbidding. One of the earliest of these stories deals with the tragic fate of young Nancy Barton, another of Colonel Whipple's servants. Nancy was engaged to one of the colonel's farmhands and had arranged to go to Portsmouth with him to be married. While she was at Lancaster, purchasing supplies for their trip, her lover departed for the coast, taking her savings from two years' service and leaving no message for her. Stricken with grief upon learning of this deceit, she tied up a small bundle of clothing and set off late in the evening from the colonel's estate in Jefferson. The snow was deep, and she had no path but spotted trees as she made her way south toward Crawford Notch, where the colonel had a camp. Wet through to the skin and worn out from fatigue and hunger, she finally reached the camp the next morning, only to find that her husband-to-be had already left. Still determined to overtake him she pressed on, but was "soon compelled to give up and sink down in utter

A pageant was held in Bethel, Maine, in 1931 to celebrate the 150th anniversary of New England's "Last Indian Raid," which took place in the upper Androscoggin River valley.

exhaustion" near a stream located at "Bemis" or "Notchland," at the southern end of Crawford Notch. Fearing for her safety, several of the colonel's workmen soon followed her into the notch, only to discover her lifeless, frozen body curled up at the foot of a tree. "The treacherous lover survived her not long," says one source, "but died in a few years, a raging maniac, in a mad-house." The sad episode is recalled today in tribute by Nancy Brook, Nancy Pond, Nancy's Bridge, and Mount Nancy.

The end of the Revolutionary War in 1783 created an environment conducive to the settlement of the White Mountain region, and hundreds of families were soon making their way into the hills in search of a new life. So rapid was this influx that the area's population increased nearly fourfold between the onset of the Revolution and the time of the first federal census in 1790. In the same way that rich intervals and virgin forests of the region now attracted scores of people who sought to improve the land by clearing it for farms and cutting trees for sawn lumber, the mountains themselves began to draw the attention of a certain class of gentlemen with a penchant for "scientific" study.

One such group, made up of a half-dozen well-educated men from Maine, Massachusetts, and New Hampshire, gathered in Conway in July of 1784 to carry out a tour of the White Mountains "with a view to make particular observations on the several phenomena which might occur." Armed with a sextant, telescope, barometer, thermometer, and two surveying compasses, and led by the redoubtable John Evans of Fryeburg, this impressive contingent set out for Jackson and Pinkham Notch with the goal of ascending "the Sugar Loaf." Surviving accounts of this expedition tell us that the group, which included the historian Jeremy Belknap of Dover, and the Reverend Manasseh Cutler (an expert botanist) of Ipswich, Massachusetts, spent their first night camped out in a meadow not far from the present Pinkham Notch Visitor Center of the Appalachian Mountain Club. The next day, most of the group made their way to the top amid "clouds, which rolled up and down, in every direction, above, below, and around them," passing through Tuckerman Ravine, whose sheer headwall was described as being "like steep stairs, the rocks of different forms, wedged in by one another in various attitudes of bigness." After making "some unsatisfactory observations with the barometer" that gave a height for the mountain of nearly 10,000 feet, this party christened the grand pinnacle "Mount Washington," after the Revolutionary hero who would soon become the country's first president.

This pioneering excursion into the Presidential Range—the first well-documented mountain climb in North America—was the progenitor of many visits to these highlands by some of the country's most eminent naturalists and scientists during the late eighteenth and early nineteenth centuries. In 1804, Manasseh Cutler returned to the White Mountains to collect botanical specimens in the company of Nathaniel Bowditch and William D. Peck, two highly respected scientists of the period. Although "much chilled" during their sojourn to the top of Mount Washington, the party was able to obtain

White Mountains, N. H. Nancy Brook at Bemis.

The tragic tale of Nancy Barton is recalled in "Nancy Brook" near the southern entrance to Crawford Notch. A nearby mountain and pond also bear her name.

barometrical observations which produced a figure of 7,055 feet for the summit's elevation, a more reasonable estimate than anything produced thus far. Others who explored the mountains about this time included physician George Shattuck of Boston and noted botanists Jacob Bigelow, Francis Boott, and William Oakes, the latter of whom summarized many of his findings in one of the classic studies of the region, *Scenery of the White Mountains*, published in 1848. All of these early scientists were stimulated by a serious desire to study and record the unique natural environment here, and their descriptions of the "Alps of New England" kindled an interest in the grandeur of the region that has lasted to the present day.

The first extended and detailed descriptions of the scenery of the White Mountain region are found in the second volume of Reverend Timothy Dwight's *Travels in New England and New York*, published in 1821. President of Yale College from 1794 to 1817 and a major figure in New England during the early years of the republic, Dwight was concerned with the rapid transformation of the Northeast from a wilderness into a civilized society. His travels, and the writings stemming from them, allowed him to describe the reshaping of his country's character during the post-Revolutionary period, while at the same time correcting the misguided opinions published by foreign visitors and critics. Dwight visited the White Mountains twice, in 1797 and 1803, and was particularly taken by the "wild and solemn appearance" of Crawford Notch. During both visits, he lodged with Grafton, Massachusetts, native Eleazer Rosebrook, who had moved to a remote mountain location near present-day Fabyan Station at Bretton Woods, several miles north of the Gate of the Notch. Dwight's admiration for the steadfastness and integrity of this stalwart pioneer of the White Mountains is apparent in his published recollections:

> This man, with a spirit of enterprise, industry, and perseverance which has surmounted obstacles demanding more patience and firmness than are in many instances required for the acquisition of empire, planted himself in this spot in the year 1788. At that time there was but a single house within twenty miles. . . . Here he stationed himself in an absolute wilderness, and was necessitated to look for everything, which was either to comfort or support life, to those who lived at least twenty miles from him, and to whom he must make his way without a road. By his industry he has subdued a farm of 150, or 200 acres, and built two large barns, the very boards of which he must have transported from a great distance with such expense and difficulty as the inhabitants of older settlements would think intolerable. He has, however, had the satisfaction for some time to see these barns annually filled with the produce of his farm.
>
> He is now preparing to erect a sawmill, and after that a gristmill; and, when these are finished, he proposes to build himself a house. Hitherto

Mount Washington received its name in 1784 during the first well-documented mountain climb in North America. This 1848 lithograph shows the west side of the Presidential Range from "Giant's Grave."

he has lived in a log hut, in which he has entertained most of the persons traveling in this road during the last eight years. The number of these is very great, and but for this single man it is not easy to conceive how the road could have well been traveled. The distance between the houses previously built is so great and the region so inhospitable that travelers would always have been exposed to suffer, and in the cold season to perish, and their horses to starve, were it not that they here found the necessary shelter and supplies. . . . For the usual inconveniences of a log house we were prepared, but we found comfortable beds, good food, and excellent fare for our horses, all furnished with as much good will as if we had been near friends of the family. Our entertainment would by most Englishmen, and not a small number of Americans, be regarded with disdain. To us it was not barely comfortable; it was, in the main, pleasant.

During twelve out of fourteen years, this honest, industrious man labored on his farm without any legal title. The proprietor was an inhabitant of New York, and sold him the land through the medium of an agent. When he bought it, the agent promised to procure a deed for him speedily. Throughout this period he alternately solicited and was promised the conveyance which had been originally engaged. Nor did he resolve until he had by building and cultivation increased the value of his farm twentyfold to go in person to New York and demand a deed of the proprietor himself. The truth is, he possesses that downright, unsuspecting integrity which, even in men of superior understanding, often exposes them to imposition from a confidence honorable to themselves, but at times unhappily misplaced. Here, however, the fact was otherwise, for the proprietor readily executed the conveyance according to the terms of the original bargain. In my journey of 1803, I found Rosebrook in possession of a large, well-built farmer's house, mills, and various other conveniences, and could not help feeling a very sensible pleasure at finding his industry, patience, and integrity thus rewarded.

Eleazer Rosebrook's cabin, and later his house, stood atop an extensive glacial mound long known as the "Giant's Grave," where, in 1872, the sprawling Fabyan House hotel would be constructed. Previous to Rosebrook's occupancy, his son-in-law Abel Crawford had built a cabin here. Yet after relinquishing the property to Rosebrook, Crawford moved 12 miles down the Saco River Valley into Hart's Location, where he opened a tavern known as the Mount Crawford House. It seems clear that Rosebrook replaced Crawford's rough-hewn cabin with a larger house in preparation for the opening in 1803 of the Tenth New Hampshire Turnpike, a 20-mile improved highway running from Bartlett north through the notch. Costing some $40,000 to build, this toll road for the most part followed the route of the existing highway. "The effects of the labors of the incorporated company were soon seen in the increasing travel," wrote the Reverend Benjamin G. Willey in his 1856 work, *Incidents in White Mountain History*:

> Portland, the nearest and most accessible of the seaboard towns, was, in those days, the great market for all this part of New Hampshire. Well can we remember the long train of Coos teams which used to formerly pass through Conway. In winter, we have seen lines of teams half a mile in length; the tough, scrubby, Canadian horses harnessed to "pungs," well loaded down with pork, cheese, butter and lard, the drivers rivalling almost the modern locomotive and its more elegant train of carriages in noise and bluster.

Catering to the needs of teamsters, local farmers, and the occasional tourist, Eleazer Rosebrook has long been credited with opening "the first house for the accommodation of travelers erected in the White Mountains." Since a number of White Mountain towns were already supplied with "public houses" by 1803, perhaps it is more accurate to say that Rosebrook's modest inn was the first of its type opened in the "solitary places" in the heart of the White Mountain region.

The first map of the White Mountains to include the names of individual peaks was published in 1784 from surveys carried out from 1773 to 1774 by Captain Samuel Holland and several of his deputies. Holland's "Topographical Map of the State of New Hampshire" shows "The White Hills" (the Presidential Range) running in an almost straight line to the northwest of Conway, "The Notch" near the headwaters of the Saco River, and many of the townships that had been laid out in the Saco, Androscoggin, and Ammonoosuc River Valleys before the Revolution. These interesting details stand in marked contrast to the omission of nearly the entire western half of the White Mountain region, except for a representation of "Mooselock Mt." (Mount Moosilauke) and a line to suggest the approximate location of the upper reaches of the Pemigewasset River. Since it was not until 1793 that settlers in the Connecticut and Ammonoosuc Valleys began to agitate for improvements to the rough trail through Franconia Notch, Holland's survey team probably turned back once they encountered the impenetrable forests rising up toward the towering ridge of the Franconia Range on the east and the Cannon-Kinsman Range on the west. Limited knowledge concerning the "Franconia Mountains," in combination with the earlier fame of Mount Washington and the Presidential Range, produced varied assumptions regarding the relationship of these westernmost mountains to the better known peaks closer to the New Hampshire/Maine border, such as that expressed in 1803 by the Reverend Timothy Dwight:

> There is nothing in Bethlehem which merits notice except the patience, enterprise, and hardihood of the settlers, which have induced them to venture and stay upon so forbidding a spot, a magnificent prospect of the

White Mountains, and a splendid collection of other mountains in their neighborhood, particularly on the southwest. These are entirely separated from the White Mountains by a deep and narrow valley. Among them, one [Lafayette], inferior only to the White Mountains and Moosilauke, exhibits in its great elevation, elegance of form, and amplitude a very rare combination of beauty and grandeur. . . . As seen from the hills of Bethlehem, it appears on the right of the White Mountains, as does Pondicherry on the left.

Timothy Dwight's observations regarding the craggy summits to the south and east of 5,260-foot Mount Lafayette, originally called the "Great Haystack," represent a perception of local geography that remained popular for many years. In fact, well into the nineteenth century many people continued to regard the mountainous region between Crawford Notch and the Connecticut River as separate from the White Mountains proper—much in the way that some today look upon the Mahoosuc Range and Evans Notch area (containing 47,000 acres

Published in 1844, this is the earliest image of the Flume in Franconia Notch. The famous boulder was dislodged by a storm-caused avalanche in 1883.

of the White Mountain National Forest) as being outside the White Mountains because they lie not in New Hampshire, but in Maine.

By 1800, farmers living in towns "above" Franconia Notch had widened and improved the road leading south through that awe-inspiring mountain pass so they could drive their ox teams and horse-drawn sleds and wagons to markets in Portsmouth and Boston. Sarah N. Welch, in her *History of Franconia, New Hampshire* (1972), states that this early road was "very narrow and the branches of trees joined hands over it. One saw little or nothing of the mountains while driving through the notch, except at a few places where there were openings." This would help explain why it was not until 1805, when survey work was being conducted at the north end of the notch, that the discovery was made of the Old Man of the Mountain, the "cardinal wonder of the New Hampshire highlands." The most widely accepted version of the discovery story involves two Franconia men, Luke Brooks and Francis Whitcomb, who were running lot lines alongside the notch road that summer. One evening, with darkness coming on, the men set up camp for the night on the shore of what was then called Ferrin's Pond, and now Profile Lake. When dawn arrived, Luke Brooks went to the lake for water, and when he stood up his gaze turned to the precipitous slopes of the mountain rising from the opposite shore. As if to direct his attention, the sun's rays cast their bright light on the granite ledges high above, revealing the rugged outline of a

Romantic White Mountain scenery captured the imaginations of genteel travelers during the early nineteenth century. This view of Mount Chocorua from Lake Winnipesaukee was a particular favorite.

man's face peering out over the verdant valley. Speechless with wonder, Brooks stood in amazement for several minutes, finally turning away long enough to call out to his companion, who soon joined him. As the story goes, one of the men declared that the rock-formed profile was the spitting image of Thomas Jefferson, then President of the United States.

The discovery of the magnificent stone profile on Cannon Mountain's east face was followed around 1808 by word of yet another marvel of nature's handiwork concealed beneath the thick forest canopy just a few miles down the notch. While searching for new fishing spots along a cascading brook of crystal-clear water, 93-year-old "Aunt Jesse" Guernsey had stumbled upon the Flume, a deep fissure extending several hundred feet into the mountainside. Following the stream into this dark gorge, she found herself hemmed in by moss-covered walls of rock rising in places to a height of 70 feet. Guernsey was astounded by the appearance of this gigantic stone canyon and even more amazed to behold a mammoth, egg-shaped boulder wedged between the mighty walls and suspended high above the roaring stream like the sword of Damocles. Some have written that Guernsey was experiencing a "second childhood" at the time, which helps to explain why her description of the enormous chasm was initially doubted by neighbors. It was not until she showed the Flume to a local farm boy that her story was believed and news of this extraordinary cleft at the base of Mount Liberty began to spread throughout the surrounding countryside.

Visited today by upwards of a million people each year, Franconia Notch's "museum of natural curiosities" did not begin to attract substantial numbers of tourists and pleasure seekers until an article was published in the September 9, 1826, issue of the *New Hampshire Statesman*. This essay contained a report of an early ascent of Mount Lafayette, which probably received its name during the great French general's tour of America from 1824 to 1825. Shortly after this article appeared, the existence of the Old Man of the Mountain was made known to the world at large by General Martin Field, whose account of an 1827 visit to the Profile was published in the July 1828 issue of the *American Journal of Science and Arts*. This brief narrative about the Old Man was accompanied by an engraving "so curiously exaggerated as to be grotesque." During the 1820s, in response to a growth in traffic and the opening of an iron foundry in the town of Franconia, the Pemigewasset, Upper Coos, and Franconia Turnpikes were chartered so that substantial improvements could be made to roads leading south through the notch to Woodstock, as well as east to the town of Bethlehem.

The rise of the tourist industry in the White Mountains resulted from an intellectual exercise by people of "sophistication and good taste," whereupon the region's forbidding landscapes were gradually transformed into "sublime" mountain scenery. Following a pattern established by English travelers of the late eighteenth century, certain Americans, as well as people from abroad, began to see something more in the White Mountains than just a remote land filled with backwoods pioneers and primitive taverns. In the Alps, the Lake District of England, and the mountains of Wales, the seductive power of "romantic" scenery had already

The "cardinal wonder of the New Hampshire highlands," the Old Man of the Mountain was discovered about 1805. The Profile measures some 40 feet high from forehead to chin and is suspended 1,200 feet above the floor of Franconia Notch.

captured the imaginations of genteel travelers interested in the potential for poetic and intellectual associations. By 1816, this model from across the Atlantic was being applied to the White Mountains, as evidenced by the following text from Philip Carrigain's map of New Hampshire, published that year:

> With regard to the face of the country, its features are striking and picturesque. The natural scenery of mountains of greater elevation than any others in the United States; of lakes, of cataracts, of vallies [*sic*] furnishes a profusion of the sublime and beautiful. It may be called the Switzerland of America.

The allure of romantic mountain scenery was also a powerful antidote to what many thought was America's growing obsession with commerce and industry. Nevertheless, the Reverend Jeremy Belknap thought it best to issue this advice to White Mountain travelers in his *History of New Hampshire* (1812):

> Nature has, indeed, in that region, formed her works on a large scale, and presented to view, many objects which do not ordinarily occur. A

person who is unacquainted with a mountainous country, cannot, upon his first coming into it, make an adequate judgment of heights and distances; he will imagine every thing to be nearer and less than it really is, until, by experience, he learns to correct his apprehensions, and accommodate his eye to the magnitude and situation of the objects around him. When amazement is excited by the grandeur and sublimity of the scenes presented to view, it is necessary to curb the imagination, and exercise judgment with mathematical precision; or the temptation to romance will be invincible.

Much of what we know of early White Mountain tourism is preserved in the pages of Lucy Crawford's *History of the White Mountains*, a classic of Americana that provides a vivid account of the trials, perils, and adventures of the Crawford family, especially of leading members Abel Crawford ("the Patriarch of the Mountains") and his son Ethan Allen Crawford ("the Giant of the Hills"). Originally issued in 1846, this fascinating chronicle is told in the first person of Ethan Allen and is fortunately still in print, providing modern-day readers with a rare glimpse of the "fashionable tour" as experienced by the first generation of White Mountain tourists.

Born in 1792 in Guildhall, Vermont, Ethan Allen was raised on his parent's Saco River farmstead at the southern entrance to Crawford Notch. "Here," said historian Frederick Kilbourne, "he grew up in circumstances that made him tough and healthy." In 1811, he enlisted as a soldier for 18 months, and upon completing his term of service returned to his father's place in Hart's Location where he engaged in various occupations, such as repairing roads, river driving, and farming. His extraordinary strength was demonstrated about this time by being able to lift a barrel of potash weighing 500 pounds into a boat, after hoisting it two feet off the ground.

Ethan Allen was working in Louisville, New York, when he received word in 1816 of his grandfather Rosebrook's ill health, and at the old innkeeper's request Crawford returned to take care of his grandparents in exchange for the farm at Giant's Grave. In the fall of 1817, having moved back to assume his grandfather's duties and indebtedness, Ethan Allen married his cousin, Lucy Howe, of Lancaster. The young couple's fortitude was severely tested soon after when the old Rosebrook stand caught fire from a neglected candle and burned to the ground on July 18, 1818. Though no lives were lost, this event was a financial setback the family never recovered from. "I was young and ambitious," stated Crawford, "but this shock of misfortune almost overcame me; and I was for some days quite indifferent which way the world went." With the help of his neighbors, Crawford drew a small house he owned by ox teams from a site a mile and a half away to the ruins at Giant's Grave. It was in this modest abode, which was only 24 feet square, that the family lived and entertained travelers until an addition was made in 1825. During this time, Ethan Allen established his reputation as a skilled path builder, capable mountain guide, and fearless hunter.

Organized hiking in this country was in its infancy in 1818 when Abel and Ethan Allen were approached for the first time by visitors who wanted to be guided to the top of Mount Washington. Lucy Crawford's *History* describes this party simply as "Colonel Binney, from Boston, with two young men," who came to the notch by way of Littleton. Finding Ethan Allen's family "so destitute of everything" as a consequence of the recent fire, the three continued south through the notch to the Mount Crawford House. There, they discussed the climb with Abel, who agreed to be their guide and arrange for another man to act as porter. Early the next morning, the group of men journeyed back up through the notch by carriage, stopping near the shore of Saco Lake where they "proceeded to the woods." Though no trail then existed along the great southwesterly ridge leading to the summit of Mount Washington, Abel knew that his father-in-law, Eleazer Rosebrook, had occasionally guided curiosity-seekers across the "Southern Presidentials" and back in one day, so the possibility of success seemed likely. This first of many trips into the mountains led by members of this unique family was later recorded in the Crawford *History*:

> They had much difficulty in managing to get through; they, however, proceeded slowly; sometimes crawling under a thicket of trees, sometimes over logs and windfalls, until they arrived where they could walk on the tops of trees. This may seem to some strange, but it is nevertheless true. They never reached the summit but managed to get along on some of the hills.
>
> As the day was growing to a close, they returned to the woods, in order to pass the night, and erected a shelter for their protection. A dense fog arose and during the night it rained. In the morning, owing to the darkness, they could not tell the best way to proceed, but took the surest way, by following the Amanoosuc [*sic*] river, and came to my house. These men wore fine and costly garments into the woods, but when they returned, their clothes were torn and much injured by the brush, and their hats looked as if they had been through a beggar's press. They were much exposed all night, without fire or food.

In September of 1818, Abel was more successful when he accompanied two young men to the top of "Trinity Height," as the cone of Mount Washington was then called. These gentlemen set in the topmost rock a brass plate bearing a Latin inscription describing their trip, which they had prepared in advance. In May of the following year, Ethan Allen provided instructions to a party of four men who wished to climb Mount Washington. "They made the best they could of their excursion through the forests," stated Crawford, "but suffered considerable inconvenience by the thickness of the trees and brush." Abel and Ethan Allen may have been rugged mountain pioneers, but they also had a shrewd business sense that allowed them to foresee that an increase in summer travel would result from the development of a permanent trail up Mount Washington. Ethan later wrote:

> As this was the third party which had visited the mountains since I came here to live, we thought it best to cut a path through the woods; accordingly my father and I made a foot path from the Notch out through the woods, and it was advertised in the newspapers, and we soon began to have a few visitors.

This trail was begun late in the spring of 1819 and initially extended only as far as Mount Pierce (originally called Mount Clinton), but was ultimately lengthened to the summit of Mount Washington. Still utilized today, the now-famous "Crawford Path" holds the distinction of being the oldest continuously maintained hiking trail in North America.

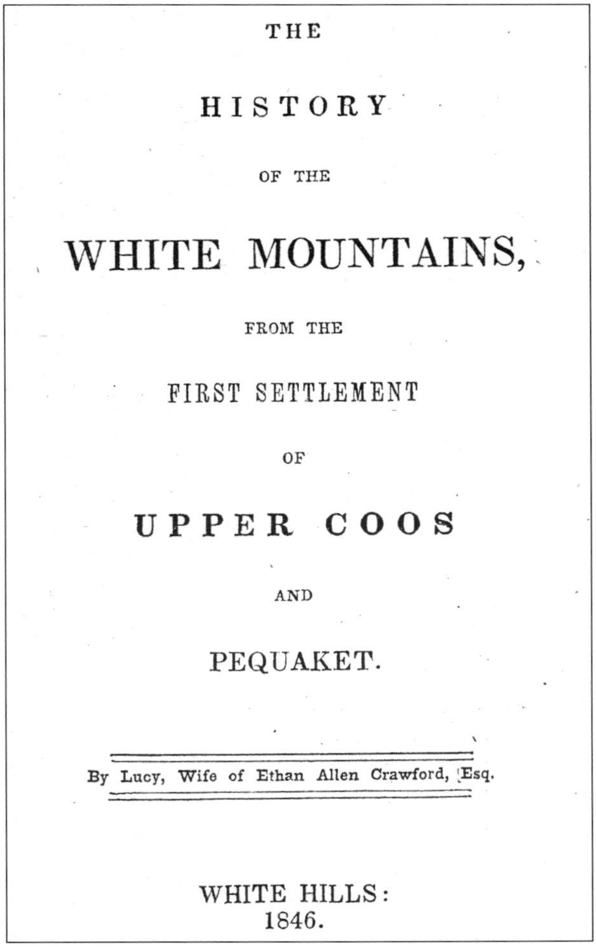

Much of what we know today of pioneer days in the White Mountains comes from Lucy Crawford's 1846 History. Several editions of this classic have been published over the years.

THE

HISTORY

OF THE

WHITE MOUNTAINS,

FROM THE

FIRST SETTLEMENT

OF

UPPER COOS

AND

PEQUAKET.

By Lucy, Wife of Ethan Allen Crawford, Esq.

WHITE HILLS:
1846.

The publication of guidebooks specific to the White Mountains was many years into the future when the Crawfords began to capitalize on their skills as path builders. But general travel guides, such as that penned by Timothy Dwight, in combination with newspaper articles, soon drew many others to the region to experience the windswept heights of the Presidential Range and to be entertained by these colorful mountain characters. One of the first parties to make use of the newly opened Crawford Path included Caleb Cushing, the jurist and Congressman, Samuel J. May, the abolitionist, and George B. Emerson, author of the highly regarded work *Trees and Shrubs of Massachusetts*. Harvard graduates all, these distinguished visitors journeyed from Kennebunk, Maine, by horseback and contracted with Abel to guide them safely up and back.

During the summer of 1820, a group of men from the nearby town of Lancaster ascended Mount Washington with the goal of naming the other peaks in the "White Mountain Range" for Presidents of the United States. With Ethan Allen as guide, and loaded with "cloaks and necessary articles" for a two-night stay, the group scrambled to the top of the mountain where they christened Mounts Adams, Jefferson, Madison, and Monroe with a plentiful quantity of "O-be-joyful." Having exhausted the list of presidents, they continued their toasts (and cheers) by naming Mounts Franklin and Pleasant (now Eisenhower). Returning to the "Presidential Range" a month later, three of the original party plus a few of their neighbors investigated the northern peaks further by climbing Jefferson, Adams, and Madison—the first recorded ascents of these mountains.

With more and more people coming to the White Mountains to take in the stunning views from the barren crown of Mount Washington, the Crawford Path's tenure as the only route up was destined to be a brief one. Consequently, in the fall of 1820 a path was opened from near Jackson "into the Glen" and thence up the eastern flank of the mountain to the summit cone. In 1824, a log hut was erected near the base of this trail as a convenience for those ascending from Pinkham Notch, but since more comfortable accommodations existed on the western side of the mountains and the road through Crawford Notch was better maintained, most tourists still preferred to climb from that direction.

Because the path he and his father had opened was out of the way for those staying at Giant's Grave, in March of 1821 Ethan Crawford hired Charles Stuart "to come with his compass and go into the woods and see if there could not be a better and more practicable way found to ascend the mountains." After three days of work, Crawford and his surveyor determined that a route alongside the Ammonoosuc River to near the present Base Station, and thence up the ridge now used by the Mount Washington Cog Railway, would be the most advantageous. That summer, Crawford and his hired men made good progress on opening this new path until a log upon which Crawford was standing broke, dropping him down with such force that the blade of his axe nearly severed the heel cord on his right foot. With the help of his men, Crawford made it back home, where he was cared for by the "old Doctress woman" Granny Stalbird, who was then visiting.

During the summer of 1820, a group of hikers ascended Mount Washington and named the other peaks in the Presidential Range. Mounts Jefferson and Adams rise above the Great Gulf in this view.

Mount Washington's powerful hold on the public imagination at this time is amply illustrated by a milestone event occurring shortly after the new trail up the west side of the mountain was completed. Ethan Crawford stated:

> On August 31, 1821, there came three young ladies, the Misses Austin, who were formerly from Portsmouth, to ascend the hills, as they were ambitious and wanted to have the honor of being the first females who placed their feet on this high and now celebrated place, Mount Washington.

Joined in this expedition by their brother and Charles Stuart, who had laid out the new path, and by a Mr. Faulkner, who was a tenant on their parents' farm in Jefferson, the sisters gradually made their way up the mountain, taking several days to reach the top and staying in small lean-to camps Ethan had provided along the way. "The ladies returned, richly paid for their trouble, after being out five days and three nights," says the Crawford *History*. This same source also alludes to the fact that mountain climbing was not yet an accepted sphere for women:

> I think this act of heroism ought to confer an honor on them, as everything was done with so much prudence and modesty by them; there

59

The opening of the Crawford Path in 1819 made it easier for climbers to reach the top of Mount Washington. The following year, another trail was built to the summit from this road in Pinkham Notch.

> was not left a trace or even a chance for a reproach or slander excepting
> by those who thought themselves outdone by these young ladies.

Like a morning mist, however, any doubts about the ability of women to climb Mount Washington, or any other high peaks in the world, would soon evaporate.

Responding to an increase in hikers, many of whom yearned to see the sunset and sunrise from the top of Mount Washington, Ethan Crawford built three small stone shelters there in July of 1823. When these proved to be too "damp and cheerless" for his guests, Crawford went to Portland and purchased a canvas tent large enough for 18 people to sleep in. Soon afterwards, he carried the 80-pound tent and a large wooden pole up the mountain to a point near the top, where a spring and a sheet-iron stove (he had placed it there before) were available. This shelter served for a time, and may have been in use as late as August 1825 when Lucy Crawford, with a gentleman and his sister from Boston, made her first trip to the summit. But violent storms, for which Mount Washington is famous, eventually tore the tent to shreds and forced visitors to return below the treeline for shelter.

Much has changed since the Crawford family first opened their doors to travelers, but one ingredient in the visitor experience has remained constant over time: certain parts of the White Mountains, and especially the summit of Mount

Washington, are home to the "world's worst weather," due to the convergence of three major storm tracks over the area. As many who ascend these ancient hills have discovered, on days when the sun is shining brightly upon the valley settlements, dense cloud cover and near hurricane-force winds can be encountered atop the higher peaks. Even within the shelter of the lower districts, mountain weather can become severe very quickly. Ethan wrote:

> The wind comes down through the narrows of the Notch with such violence that it requires two men to hold one man's hair on, as I have heard them say. . . . I have never found it to blow so hard here as to equal this, yet it has blown so hard as to take loaded sleighs and carry them several rods to a stone wall, which was frozen down so firmly that it was impenetrable, and there the sleigh stopped.

Crawford had firsthand experience in such matters, for once, when he was hauling a heavy load around a tight corner near the Gate of the Notch, a gust of wind nearly tipped his sleigh into a deep gulf, horses and all. Bracing his feet against the railing on the road, he held the load back until the wind abated and then righted the sleigh by pushing hard with his shoulder. Little wonder he was known as "the Giant of the Hills." Not surprisingly, most of Ethan Crawford's recollections of adverse weather in the mountains are linked to the upper reaches of Mount Washington. One example, preserved in Lucy Crawford's *History*, is particularly striking:

> Again, we had another party come, from which I will relate a circumstance. We went up the mountain, the weather then looking favorable, until we reached the top of the hill, and then we went into a cloud, which was dark all around us. Having reached the summit, and not having any landmarks to direct us back, and not being acquainted with the weather here, we staid only long enough for them to carve their names, and then tried to return; but I was lost, myself, for a short time. I started toward the east, and we wandered about until we came near the edge of a great gulf. Here we staid and amused ourselves by rolling such large stones as we could find loose, and these being started, went with such force that they would take others with them, and then rest only in the valley beneath. Although a little danger was encountered in this kind of sport, had one of us slipped accidentally and been precipitated down the gulf, yet it was actually a grand sight.

Casting boulders down the steep sides of Mount Washington seems to have been one of many ways these early hikers amused themselves. One of Ethan Crawford's favorite stories told around the campfire involved the thunder-like noises caused by landslides on the Presidential Range, which frightened the native population so that they refused to visit the cloud-capped peaks to investigate. Yet young Crawford and others who lived year-round in the mountains knew well the dangers associated with landslides that were not of the man-made type. In the late spring of 1826, the "Old Patriarch" Abel Crawford was at work with several other men in the notch, repairing the Tenth New Hampshire Turnpike, when a downpour took place. "While there they saw on the west side of the road a small movement of rocks and earth coming down the hill, and it took all before it," recalled Ethan Crawford. "They saw whole trees coming down, standing upright, for ten rods together, before they would tip over—the whole still moving slowly on, making its way until it had crossed the road." This "grand and awful sight" frightened the family of Samuel Willey Jr., who had taken up residence in a nearby house erected about 1793 in the heart of the narrow defile as a shelter for travelers. As the sun returned to the sky and the workmen got back to their labors, Samuel Willey stared at his modest home tucked closely under the great mountain forming the western wall of the notch. The stillness of the day helped calm his fears, and he resumed his chores, little imagining that the fate of his family and his home would soon draw a nation's attention to the White Mountains.

Mount Washington's summit is frequently hidden by clouds. While waiting for the sun to appear, early hikers amused themselves by rolling large boulders down the mountain to cause landslides.

5. THE HEROIC ERA

The summer of 1826 was to be a memorable one in northern New England. The spring rains were followed by many weeks of unusually high temperatures and a prolonged drought that dried the thin soils of the upland regions into a fine powder. Along the broad intervals in the Saco, Connecticut, and Androscoggin River Valleys, farmers watched helplessly as their crops withered under a fervid sun. In the many villages that now dotted the White Hills, clouds of dust rose slowly into the air each time a horse-drawn wagon passed through. Despite these arid conditions, it seemed to Ethan Crawford and other local innkeepers that the number of visitors coming to the mountains had increased over the previous year.

During the final week of August, dark clouds foretelling rain at last began to gather over the mountains. The appearance of these clouds left the Reverend Benjamin G. Willey of Conway with an unsettled feeling, especially when he thought about his brother's family living in the depths of Crawford Notch. "I had often seen storms gather in the regions of those compacted and elevated mountains, but never before with such grandeur and awfulness," wrote the reverend in his 1856 work, *Incidents in White Mountain History*. Spreading over the mountains like a "dark solemn drapery," the thunderclouds reminded him of "some heavy armed legions moving slowly and steadily to battle." Willey's imaginings, as it turned out, were not far from the truth.

Early in the evening of August 28, the rain began to fall, increasing in its intensity until around 11:00 p.m. when "it seemed as though the windows of heaven were opened and the rain came down almost in streams," recalled Ethan Allen Crawford. Amid the flashes of lightning and loud peals of thunder, there could be heard the concussion of rocks on the mountain sides reverberating through the night air as though trying to compete with the deafening roar of the rain that was now falling in torrents. By midnight, the sky had cleared and the moon shone brightly, throwing a strange half-light on a landscape transformed by the power of nature's fury.

In the morning, Ethan Crawford was awakened by his little boy, who exclaimed, "Father, the earth is nearly covered with water, and the hogs are swimming for life." Stepping outside, Crawford was shocked by what he saw.

All around his farm the valley was a "vast ocean" of water, fed by rushing streams that had cut deep grooves into the mountains. As Crawford soon learned, all of the bridges on the turnpike through Crawford Notch had been demolished, save two; the road through Franconia Notch had fared no better, with whole sections utterly destroyed. Abel Crawford had been away at the time of the storm, leaving his wife Hannah to defend the Mount Crawford House from the rising waters; this she did by standing in a second floor window with a long pole and pushing away floating debris as it accumulated against the building. Staring north from his home in Conway, Reverend Willey was astounded by the changes the morning after the tempest: "I never saw such in all my life . . . it was judged that more destruction of trees, and more displacing of rocks and earth, were made on that terrible night than had been made since the country was settled." Fearing for the safety of his brother's family, Willey began making inquiries and remained somewhat hopeful, but on Wednesday evening word came from his physician, Dr. Chadbourne, in Bartlett that the whole family had been lost.

In a matter of a few days, friends and relatives of the Willeys made their way into the notch to search for the family. The scene around the deserted Willey house was one of utter desolation and ruin, but even more astonishing was how much of the mountain above and behind the house had broken free and plunged to the valley floor. This great avalanche had come directly toward the

The famous "Willey Disaster" of August 1826 brought national attention to the White Mountains when the Willey House miraculously survived a landslide that destroyed its occupants.

home, but upon reaching a low ridge behind it, had separated into two channels, carrying away the stable and reuniting a short distance in front of the dwelling. Inside the house were indications of a rapid departure—unmade beds, ashes in the fireplace, and clothes lying in chairs and on the floor. Yet what had happened to its occupants? The Crawford *History* relates the grim discovery of the family's remains:

> Diligent search being made for them, and no traces to be found until night, the attention of the people was attracted by the flies as they were passing and repassing underneath a large pile of floodwood. They now began to haul away the rubbish and at length found Mr. and Mrs. Willey, Mr. Allen, the hired man, and the youngest child not far distant from each other. These were taken up, broken and mangled, as must naturally be expected, and were placed in coffins. . . . Saturday, the other hired man was found and interred, and on Sunday the eldest daughter was found, some way from where the others were, across the river.

After the victims of the "Willey Disaster" were temporarily buried near the house (three of the children were never found), members of the rescue party began to develop theories to explain the household's movements that dreadful night. Struggling to understand what had led his brother's family to hasten from the house to their deaths, Benjamin G. Willey offered various rationales in his *Incidents in White Mountain History*, published 30 years later. The most commonly accepted explanation was set forth in Willey's book as follows:

> The family, at first, designed to keep the house, and did actually remain in it till after the descent of most of the slides. From the commencement of the storm in its greatest fury they were, probably, on the alert, though previously to this some of them might have retired to rest. That the children had, was pretty evident from appearances in the house when first entered after the disaster. My brother, it is pretty certain, had not undressed; he stood watching the movements and vicissitudes of the awfully anxious season. When the storm had increased to such violence as to threaten their safety, and descending avalanches seemed to be sounding "the world's last knell," he roused his family and prepared them, as he could, for a speedy flight, trembling every moment lest they should be buried under the ruins of their falling habitation.
>
> At this hurried, agitating moment of awful suspense, the slide, which parted back of the house, is supposed to have come down, a part of which struck and carried away the stable. Hearing the crash, they instantly and precipitately rushed from their dwelling, and attempted to flee in the opposite direction. But the thick darkness covering all objects from their sight, they were almost instantly engulfed in the

After the 1826 catastrophe, the Willey House evolved into a major American tourist attraction. Each summer, thousands of people visited Crawford Notch to see this cultural icon.

desolating torrent which passed below the house, and which precipitated them, together with rocks and trees, into the swollen and frantic tide below, and cut off at once all hope of escape. Amidst the rage and foam of so much water, filled, as it was, with so many instruments of death, they had no alternative but the doom which was before them.

News of the catastrophe spread rapidly throughout the region, thanks in part to wide coverage in many of New England's most prominent papers, so that by the fall of 1826 hundreds of people were flocking to the mountains to view the Willey House and its dramatic setting. Many travelers to the site agreed with Benjamin Silliman, one of the leading American scientists of the day, when he called the event "*almost* a miracle," referring to the fact that the slide had encircled the house, but still destroyed the family. At the time of the Willey Disaster, well-to-do Americans were anxious to visit places infused with religious and nationalistic symbolism, and the providential sparing of the Willey "home" satisfied these impulses perfectly. No longer restricted to views of Old World ruins to gratify their "craving for catastrophe," Americans now had their own ruins amid a setting as sublime and "terrible" as anything in Europe. As a result, in just a few years time, thousands of people were making pilgrimages to the White Mountains to tour the Willey House and bask in the Gothic-like dreariness of the notch. The principal inspiration for early White Mountain literature and art, the Willey Disaster produced one of America's first major tourist attractions.

The great storm of 1826 had done irreparable damage to Ethan Allen Crawford's farm and increased his debts substantially, but the people of Portland, Maine, eased his worries and those of his neighbors somewhat by raising $1,500 to help repair the road through Crawford Notch. Encouraged by this sign of support, the turnpike directors managed to make up the balance, and repairs were begun in September. "We all went to work," exclaimed Crawford, "and, as it was said, the sun shone so short a time in this Notch, that the hardy New Hampshire boys made up their hours by moonlight." Favored with good weather, the work crew had progressed considerably by the time snow fell, and a decent sleigh path was available to travelers that winter. In other districts of the White Mountain region, similar road repairs were taking place that fall as a consequence of the "Great Freshet."

The effect of the "great and wonderful catastrophe" of 1826 on the White Mountain tourist trade was instantaneous and impressive. During the summer of 1827, large numbers of visitors came to Crawford Notch to view the Willey House, to place a stone on the spot where some of the victims had been found, and to gaze upon the scarred battlements of "Mount Willey," as the 4,000-foot peak forming the western wall of the notch was now dubbed. That season, Ethan Crawford's "Old Moosehorn Tavern" was filled to capacity with guests including an interesting collection of writers, artists, scientists, and adventurers.

To entertain his visitors after they explored the notch or hiked into the mountains, Crawford told stories, hosted evening dances, and blew a large tin horn or set off a cannon to produce reverberating echoes. Members of the urban elite, eager to escape the oppressive heat in east coast cities, found Crawford's unpretentious amusements to their liking since they reinforced the image of the White Mountains as an untamed wilderness. Catering to the expectations of these wealthy and educated guests, Crawford set up pens outside his tavern where he kept a live deer, moose, bear, and wolf.

Among Crawford's visitors in 1827 was the young New York artist Thomas Cole, a founding member of the National Academy of Design and the first of many artists who would make use of the grand scenery in the White Mountains to bolster their careers. Cole, who would return to the area again in 1828 with the New Hampshire–born painter Henry Cheever Pratt, had undertaken the trip to Crawford Notch at the urging of his patron, Daniel Wadsworth of Hartford, Connecticut. Like other artists who came to the White Mountains in the 1820s and 1830s, Cole was mesmerized by the story of the avalanche and the undefinable power of nature.

Making a series of sketches on site, Cole completed two paintings in his New York studio several months later that conveyed his vision of the sublime: *View of the White Mountains*, now in the Wadsworth Athenaeum in Hartford, and *Distant View of the Slides That Destroyed the Whilley* [sic] *Family*, a now-lost image whose main focus was the precipitous slopes of Mount Willey. Considered the founder of the "Hudson River School" of artists, Cole joined Pratt in climbing Mount Chocorua in 1828, where he received the inspiration for two more scenes, *Autumn Scene—Corway Peak* and *The Death of Chocorua*, the latter made famous through a much-circulated steel engraving.

During this second visit, Cole journeyed through Franconia Notch where he viewed the Old Man of the Mountain. "While there was a pleasure in the discovery, a childish fear came over me that drove me away; the bold and horrid features, that bent their severe expression upon me, were too dreadful to look upon in my loneliness," he later wrote. Thomas Cole returned to the area in 1839, producing his well-known painting, *The Notch of the White Mountains*, which acknowledges man's taming of the wilderness by showing one of the Crawford taverns set in a recently cut out opening in the woods and surrounded by the magnificent landscape at the Gate of the Notch.

Besides Henry Cheever Pratt, other artists who visited the White Mountains about this time included Thomas Doughty, Alvan T. Fisher, Daniel Wadsworth, and William Henry Bartlett, a British illustrator who toured the area in 1836 in order to make drawings of mountains, waterfalls, gorges, and the Willey House. Bartlett's romanticized images of the White Mountains were later converted into engravings and serially published by George Virtue of London from 1838 to 1842 in the book *American Scenery*, a deluxe travelogue with text by the New York writer Nathaniel Parker Willis. In the introduction to this highly popular volume—the most widely distributed and influential collection of American landscape views published in the nineteenth century—Willis wrote:

> The interest, with regard to both the natural and civilized features of America, has very much increased within a few years; and travellers, who have exhausted the unchanging countries of Europe, now turn their steps in great numbers to the novel scenery, and ever-shifting aspects of this.

One of William H. Bartlett's drawings, "The Notch-House," illustrates what effect greater numbers of travelers were having on the limited accommodations then available in the vicinity of Crawford Notch and Bretton Woods. Lucy Crawford's *History* describes the planning behind the opening of this important forerunner of the "grand hotels" of the White Mountains:

> It now became needful for the benefit of the company, as it increased, to have an establishment at the top of the Notch, as many wanted to stop there and leave their horses and pursue their way down the hill on foot to view the cascades as they come majestically down the hill and over the rocks and form such a beautiful silvery sight. The flume, likewise, that is curiously cut out by nature through a solid rock, the avalanches, and then the Willey House, etc. On their return they needed refreshment, and having a disposition to accommodate the

public, and feeling a little self-pride to have another Crawford settled here . . . I consulted with my father, and we agreed to build there and place a brother of mine in the house.

Situated just north of the Gate of the Notch, in the shadow of the unique rock formation known as "Elephant's Head," the Notch House stood 120 feet in length and 36 in width, and opened in January 1829 under the management of Thomas J. Crawford, another of Abel Crawford's sons. Like his father and more famous brother, Tom catered to his visitors' needs by providing tastefully furnished rooms, ample meals, a post office, and "good horses and carriages" for trips around the mountains. In no time at all, the Notch House became "a great place of resort" for summer tourists, many of whom learned about the locality through widely-circulated lithographic reproductions of the Bartlett view by Isaac Sprague for William Oakes's *Scenery of the White Mountains* (1848), and by Currier and Ives (1860). About 1845, the hostelry's overnight capacity was increased to 75 guests by lengthening the building by one third and adding a series of small bedrooms in the attic story.

If the tree-clad slopes and lofty summits of the White Mountains captivated the imaginations of artists, they also served as a source of

A growing tourist trade resulted in the opening of the Notch House in 1829. This small hotel stood below "Elephant's Head" at the Gate of the Notch.

69

inspiration to writers and poets, among them Washington Irving, Ralph Waldo Emerson, Nathaniel Hawthorne, Lucy Larcom, and John Greenleaf Whittier. Although Irving referred to the mountains in a letter to his brother as "beautiful beyond expectation," little record of his July 1832 visit has survived except for a brief reference to his climb up Mount Washington in company with the English traveler Charles Joseph Latrobe. The latter wrote that they achieved the summit "under disadvantageous circumstances," but "after some hours' toil and much expectation, we were enveloped in heavy mist, which set our patience at defiance, and sent us cold and wet on our downward route."

Emerson visited the White Mountains in the same month as Irving, preaching at a church in Conway and staying at Ethan Allen Crawford's a few days later. He appreciated the benefits derived from withdrawing to the hills, but, like his friend Henry David Thoreau, who visited the White Mountains in 1839 and 1858 (spraining his ankle while exploring Tuckerman Ravine on the second trip), Emerson scorned the trappings of tourism and preferred the "quieter beauties" of the Monadnock region in southwestern New Hampshire.

One of the most popular poets of her day, Lucy Larcom began visiting the region in 1861, staying in Campton and West Ossipee at first, but relocating to Bethel at the eastern edge of the mountains during the late 1870s and 1880s. Her close friend John Greenleaf Whittier spent many vacations in the highlands from the 1840s to around 1890. Among his many poems inspired by these visits was "The White Mountains," which appeared in his first book, *Legends of New England* (1831). A 2,000-foot mountain near the village of West Ossipee is named in his memory.

Of the aforementioned writers, it was the melancholy Nathaniel Hawthorne who most fully communicated the character of the White Mountains to the American public. Hawthorne's first encounter with the White Hills took place in the fall of 1832 when he toured the heart of the region on an excursion that also took him to Lake Champlain, Lake Ontario, and Niagara Falls, the ultimate tourist stop in the nineteenth century. During mid-September, Hawthorne stayed at Ethan Allen Crawford's Old Moosehorn Tavern, climbed Mount Washington, and visited Franconia Notch, where he saw the "marvelous countenance" that would furnish the subject of his allegorical tale "The Great Stone Face," published in *The National Era* in 1850.

Hawthorne's brooding temperament, which caused him to view the tourist culture with skepticism, influenced many of his literary works dealing with the White Mountains, including "The Ambitious Guest," a story of the Willey Disaster, and "The Great Carbuncle," involving the search for buried treasure among the hills. Ironically, in May of 1864, Hawthorne passed away in one of the region's most popular tourist hotels, the Pemigewasset House at Plymouth, while traveling with his college-mate and lifelong friend, ex-President Franklin Pierce.

Among others of note visiting the White Mountains at this time were a handful of prominent scientists and politicians who wished to make a closer inspection of

White Mountain House, Fabyan, N. H.

Once operated by Ethan Allen Crawford, the White Mountain House stood north of Giant's Grave until the 1920s. The hotel's porch was equipped with a good supply of chairs for summer guests.

the famed heights. Chief among the latter was the great nineteenth century orator and United States senator from New Hampshire, Daniel Webster, who hired Ethan Allen Crawford in June of 1831 to guide him to the top of Mount Washington. Finding the summit enveloped in its usual blanket of clouds, Webster supposedly made this address:

> Mount Washington, I have come a long distance, have toiled hard to arrive at your summit, and now you seem to give me a cold reception, for which I am extremely sorry, as I shall not have time enough to view this grand prospect which now lies before me, and nothing prevents but the uncomfortable atmosphere in which you reside!

Living up to its reputation, the mountain also provided the climbers with a snowstorm, "the snow freezing on them and causing them to suffer until they had got some distance down." Crawford's disappointment in not obliging his guest with the panorama from the top was eased somewhat when Webster handed him a twenty-dollar gratuity as he departed. Years later, the 3,910-foot peak (originally "Notch Mountain") forming the eastern rampart of Crawford Notch was renamed for this great statesman.

Interest in the natural phenomena of the White Mountains continued to draw major figures from the American scientific community to the region during the

"Age of Jackson," from the late 1820s through the mid-1840s. The distinguished geologist and chemist Professor Benjamin Silliman of Yale made at least two excursions to the mountains, in 1828 and again in 1837. Silliman published his findings in the highly influential *American Journal of Science and Arts*, of which he was the founder and editor. On his first visit, the scientist approached the region by way of Concord, Center Harbor, and Conway, procuring a carriage in the latter town for the journey through Crawford Notch. Like many who were encountering the White Mountains for the first time, Silliman perceived the area through the eyes of a tourist as well. He wrote:

> We have this day passed the grandest scenes that I have any where seen.
> The whole day's ride, in an open wagon, has been in the winding defile
> of mountains, which probably have not their equal in North America,
> until we reach the Rocky Mountains.

Such remarks suggest that if the White Mountains were no longer considered the country's highest peaks, they still had the ability to astound even the most serious-minded visitors. Among other scientists who came to collect specimens of plants and minerals at this time were botanists James W. Robbins and Professor Edward Tuckerman. A professor of botany at Amherst College from 1858 to 1886, Tuckerman is remembered in the great ravine on the east side of Mount Washington. A small group of European scientists also visited the mountains about this time; among them were Swiss geologist Louis Agassiz (for whom a mountain between the villages of Franconia and Bethlehem is named) and the English geologist and botanist Sir Charles Lyell (whose 1845 visit focused on the alpine species of plants on Mount Washington and the effect of glacial movement over the area's many exposed ledges).

Perhaps the most interesting "scientific" investigation of this period was a comprehensive inventory of New Hampshire's natural resources that took place between 1840 and 1843, and involved much field work in the White Mountains. Authorized by the state legislature, this survey was directed by Dr. Charles T. Jackson of Boston, a highly respected chemist and mineralogist who received an appointment as State Geologist based on his similar examinations of Nova Scotia and Rhode Island. Jackson's assistants, who did much of the survey work itself, included a young Edward Everett Hale and Josiah Dwight Whitney, who later became a famous geologist and directed the California State Survey.

Jackson's findings were summarized in a publication entitled *Final Report on the Geology and Mineralogy of the State of New Hampshire* (1844), which featured five full-page lithographic plates of White Mountain scenes drawn by Whitney, including the first representation of the Flume in Franconia Notch. Although many of Jackson's findings were considered obsolete by the time a second state survey was carried out between 1868 and 1872, his *Report* was considered substantial enough that his name was given to one of the peaks in the Southern Presidentials.

Early White Mountain tourism was stimulated by the work of artists and writers. Nathaniel Hawthorne's allegorical tale, "The Great Stone Face," was published in 1850.

The influx of tourists into the White Mountains and the social and economic expansion of the region's towns during the 1820s and 1830s brought a greater need for improved roads and more convenient routes into and out of the mountains. One of the important highways rebuilt during this era was the so-called "Coos Road," which ran between Colebrook and Hallowell, Maine (a distance of 90 miles), and connected people in the northernmost reaches of the Connecticut River Valley with the navigable waters of the Kennebec. Opened about 1805, this road traversed the craggy pass known as Dixville Notch, where a modest inn operated by farmer John Whittemore was in place by 1812. Timothy Dwight anticipated the future popularity of this location, now the site of a grand hotel called The Balsams, after a visit in 1803 when he wrote, "The range of the White Mountains opens here a gap resembling the notch [Crawford Notch], presenting scenery finely romantic, and allowing a convenient passage for a road." Yet in a land where many people still relied on farming for their main source of

The Coos Road was laid out through Dixville Notch in 1805. At the Notch's west end is The Balsams, a grand hotel from the mid-1860s that still functions today.

income, keeping roads in good repair could be a financial, as well as a physical, challenge, as suggested by this passage from James Jackson's 1905 *History of Littleton, New Hampshire*:

> In these years, as subsequently, the town was frequently called into court to answer to complaints for not keeping the highway known as the county road in passable form. This road, like most others of the period, built along ridges and over high land, was very crooked, and its path only sufficient in width for the passage of a team. . . . It was rocky, full of roots, and in places unbridged. Many hundreds of dollars had been expended upon it, though labor was cheap—eight cents an hour for a man and four shillings and sixpence a day for a yoke of oxen.

With the advent of rail transportation into the region still some years away, and notwithstanding the availability of several "turnpikes" receiving regular maintenance work, travelers continued to endure rough roads, cramped stages, and long rides in order to reach their destinations. In 1823, a trip from Boston to Crawford Notch averaged four days; ten years later, it still took 18 hours to travel by stage from Concord to Conway. Many sojourns to the White Mountains began in Boston and involved one of two routes. The first went to Concord, and thence to Center Harbor or Meredith, and on to Conway. The other was to Portland by water and then by stage through the Maine towns of Gorham, Baldwin, Hiram, and Fryeburg. For those interested in the western district of the mountains and Franconia Notch, "post roads" led directly north from Concord to Plymouth, where overnight accommodations were available at Webster's Tavern, which was enlarged and reopened in 1841 as the first Pemigewasset House.

Because these journeys were of several days' duration, numerous village inns came into existence throughout the White Mountains, as well as in towns to the south and east, to serve tourists and other travelers. Just over the border in Maine, the three-and-a-half story Bethel House, erected by Jedediah Burbank in 1833, was one such hostelry that served local traffic as well as people utilizing the Portland-to-Lancaster stage before the railroad's arrival in Bethel in 1851. Among similar establishments opened about the same time were the Pequawket House at Conway, McMillan House and Washington House at North Conway, Blair's Hotel in Campton, Pendexter House at Intervale (Lower Bartlett), Oxford House in Fryeburg, and the Lary House in Gorham.

The early focus of White Mountain tourism had been the west side of the Presidential Range, but by the 1830s the popularity of the Old Man of the Mountain and the Flume were beginning to draw some visitors away from

The Lary House at Gorham, New Hampshire, was an important forerunner of the grand hotels in the White Mountains. The building opened in the mid-1830s and burned in 1907.

White Mts. N.H. Jefferson, Presidential Range from the Highland Road.

The Pinkham Notch road was rebuilt in the 1820s so towns north of the Presidential Range could have better access to Conway. Here we see the view south from Jefferson.

Crawford Notch and the western flank of Mount Washington to the spectacular scenery in Franconia Notch. In response to this competition, Thomas J. Crawford tried to make the trip up Mount Washington easier by converting the Crawford Path into a bridle path. In 1840, Crawford's 75-year-old father, Abel, had the honor of being the first person to ascend the mountain on horseback. Times were changing, however, and fashionable tourists were also starting to take notice of the majestic landscapes north of Jackson, between the Presidential and the Carter-Moriah Ranges.

In 1824, the prosperous farming and lumbering community of Durand, on Gorham's western border, was incorporated as Randolph. Full of pride at achieving "town" status, Randolph's citizens approached the state legislature to see if a more convenient route south could be opened through the mountains to connect with the towns of the Ellis and Saco River Valleys. Since 1774, a rough cart path—little more than a blazed trail in some places—had existed through the Eastern Pass, now Pinkham Notch. Yet for most of the intervening years, the people of Randolph and other communities north of the Presidential Range had reached Conway and Fryeburg via Jefferson and Crawford Notch, or through Shelburne, Gilead, and Bethel before heading south.

Wisely, the state legislature understood the economic advantages connected with reopening the Eastern Pass, and contracted Daniel Pinkham of Jackson to construct the 12-mile road in exchange for a grant of land on both sides of the thoroughfare. Steep and winding, but wide enough to accommodate wagons carrying freight or passengers, the road was completed over a period of several years. Daniel Pinkham received a narrow strip of land starting near Glen Ellis Falls and running north to a spot near the entrance to the present Mount Washington Auto Road.

As predicted, the road through "Pinkham's Woods" or "Pinkham's Notch" was much used for through traffic and by increasing numbers of pleasure seekers anxious to explore the sublime scenery on the east side of Mount Washington. For the first few years of the new road's existence, there was no place where travelers could get a meal or spend the night in the notch area, but by the mid-1830s word began to spread of the comfortable beds and good food to be had at the only farm between Jackson and Randolph. For the next 50 years, the rustic home of Hayes and Dolly Copp would welcome countless visitors who reveled in the forthrightness of these pioneers of "The Glen."

Born in 1804 just over the state line in Stow, Maine, Hayes Dodifer Copp spent his early manhood in the towns of Bartlett and Jackson, where he learned of the availability of prime farmland at the northern entrance of Pinkham Notch. Sometime around 1827, Copp set out for Martin's Grant with a small pack on his back, a long-barreled flintlock over his shoulder, and an axe in his hand. By the time of his marriage in 1831 to Dolly Emery of Bartlett, Copp had built a log house and cleared land enough to raise impressive crops of wheat, barley, and oats. Some of this harvest was sent off to Concord as partial payment to the state for his farmstead. Yet like the Crawfords before them, the Copps soon discovered the

The Dolly Copp Campground is the largest in the White Mountain National Forest. It occupies the old Copp farmstead at the northern edge of Pinkham Notch.

financial advantages of catering to the needs of curious travelers. The historian George N. Cross of Randolph wrote in 1927:

> Keen-eyed Dolly quickly saw the significance of the coming of city folks. . . .
> Travelers in either direction usually stopped for a meal, or, if they arrived
> late, spent the night. . . . The price of entertainment was not exorbitant—
> "a shilling all round," that is, twenty-five cents for a meal, the same for a
> bed for each person, and a quarter for the feed and care of a horse.

Hayes and Dolly Copp continued to take in a few guests even after grand hotels were built nearby in the 1850s; in fact, Dolly's woolen homespun, golden butter, rich cheese, and maple syrup were sold to guests at the nearby Glen House after that hotel opened its doors in 1852. However, after a half century of marriage and four children, the Copps surprised all who knew them by deciding to go their separate ways. Said Dolly of this mutual decision, "Hayes is well enough. But fifty years is long enough for a woman to live with any man." Leaving their home to their son, Nathaniel, the Copps moved away from the notch; Hayes went to his native town of Stow and Dolly to her daughter's home in Auburn, Maine. Today, the Dolly Copp Campground, the largest in the White Mountain National Forest, occupies the old farmstead of Hayes and Dolly Copp.

Called the "founder of the White Mountain grand hotel," Horace Fabyan built this mountain hostelry next to the Willey House in 1844. Mount Willey rises steeply in the background.

The phenomenal growth of White Mountain tourism in the 1830s and 1840s was the product of a number of factors, including changing attitudes toward recreation and nature, the creation of an American middle class with leisure time and money to spend, and shrewd marketing on the part of entrepreneurs who wanted to establish a profitable resort culture in the "Switzerland of America." During this era of heightened interest in the highlands of western Maine and northern New Hampshire, well-bred visitors continued to interpret the White Mountains as a romantic frontier, unspoiled by the hand of man. That perception, of course, had less to do with reality than with an imagined world created by, and for, people wishing to escape from a rapidly industrializing society. What mattered most to this new wave of visitors who came for longer periods of time was that they see all of the most popular locations while being entertained in settings rivaling those in such fashionable resorts as Saratoga Springs, the Catskills, and Niagara Falls. Thanks to the managerial skills of a second generation of White Mountain innkeepers, many of whom came from the same urban areas as their guests, all of this and more would soon be possible.

The transition from rustic taverns to stylish hotels in the region is perhaps best illustrated by the entrepreneurial activities of Horace Fabyan, who has been called the "founder of the White Mountain grand hotel." A native of Scarboro, Maine, Fabyan worked as a provisions dealer in Portland before marrying Miriam Eaton of Conway in 1834. By 1836, he was operating an inn at Conway, and it was there that he probably heard about an opportunity to manage Ethan Allen Crawford's Moosehorn Tavern. Records show that in the summer of 1832, Crawford mortgaged his property and added a two-story wing to the tavern in order to compete with another small hotel, the White Mountain House, which had opened a few miles north where the Cherry Mountain Road led off toward Jefferson. Beset by debt and suffering from ill health, Crawford found himself unable to make payments to a Concord bank and was forced in 1837 to sell out to three men who had been sureties on the mortgage. This sad event caused him to lament, "I expressed a regret to leave the place where we had performed so much hard labor, and had done everything to make the mountain scenery fashionable."

With the experience of inn-keeping at Conway under his belt, Horace Fabyan initially rented the Crawford stand, but by 1841 purchased the well-known hostelry and made numerous repairs, renaming it the Mount Washington House. On a tip that the railroad would be entering the mountains in a matter of a few years, Fabyan soon afterwards started construction on a three-story wing to this hotel using capital from his Portland ventures. This new section, according to the 1846 edition of *The White Mountain and Winnepissiogee Lake Guide Book*, featured "a superb dining room 60 feet in length, beautifully carpeted and curtained." Arranged in long rows above this dining room and throughout the upper floors were "chambers" for nearly 150 guests, making Fabyan's establishment one of the largest of its type in the mountains. A former guest, writing for an 1895 edition of *The White Mountain Echo*, a tourist newspaper published for many years in

The Lafayette House opened in Franconia Notch in 1835. Many of its guests came to see the nearby Old Man of the Mountain.

Bethlehem, recalled life at the Mount Washington House right after it was taken over by Fabyan:

> The rate in 1837 was $1.50 a day. The price of the trip up Mount Washington was $3. This included the services of Mr. Fabyan's cousin, Oliver Fabyan, as guide, and the use of horses, which were taken to a point three miles below the summit. A custom, begun by Mr. Crawford, of exhibiting for the pleasure of guests the remarkable echo to be heard at the Giant's Grave, was a feature of the entertainment at the Mount Washington House.

Horace Fabyan's success at attracting well-to-do couples and families to his Mount Washington House led him to purchase the old Willey House property at Crawford Notch in 1844. In that year, he built a two-and-a-half story hotel measuring 70 by 40 feet just south of the house made famous by the 1826 landslide, and after refurbishing the latter as a tourist attraction, sold both buildings to John Davis of Conway.

Horace Fabyan's Mount Washington House set the tone for fashionable hotel-keeping in the heart of the White Mountains up until its destruction by fire in

1853, but it was not the earliest forerunner of the grand hotels in the region. Besides the previously mentioned White Mountain House, which was in business by 1843, the Lafayette House in Franconia Notch, opened in 1835, falls into this category. The first inn for travelers in Franconia Notch was erected around 1830 just south of the entrance into the Flume. Known as Knight's Tavern, this hostelry was "a small affair" still in business as late as 1847, when it was mentioned briefly in a tourist guide book. Construction of the competing Lafayette House, located a few hundreds yards to the southeast of the present Cannon Mountain Aerial Tramway parking lot, permitted its proprietors, Stephen C. and Joseph L. Gibb, to take advantage of increasing numbers of travelers interested in viewing the nearby Old Man of the Mountain.

A sketch of the Lafayette House dating from 1845 shows it looking much like a farmhouse, but by the time a lithograph of the building appeared three years later in Oakes' *Scenery of the White Mountains*, a major expansion had taken place. By some estimates, this early hotel in Franconia Notch was said to have accommodated up to 50 guests. A famous personality who visited here a few months after the hotel opened was the noted English writer Harriet Martineau, who was most comfortably entertained "at Gibb's house" while on her two-year tour through the United States.

About the time the Lafayette House was being remodeled, another good-sized hotel opened further down the notch at the entrance to the Flume and the Pool. Purchased in 1849 by Richard Taft of Barre, Vermont, the first Flume House was a long, three-and-a-half story structure with an impressive colonnade running

By the 1840s, the White Mountains had become America's "most accessible wilderness." This somewhat stylized view shows Franconia Notch from the south.

across the front. Taft approached operating the Flume House with experience gained from an earlier stint as proprietor of the Washington House at Lowell, Massachusetts, and, like Horace Fabyan, introduced modern improvements that helped set it apart from the wayside taverns of the first generation of White Mountain innkeepers. A man of "exceedingly quiet demeanor, but of great ability, foresight, and cautious energy," Richard Taft was later remembered by historian Frederick W. Kilbourne as someone:

> whom the Franconia Notch region in particular and New Hampshire in general owes a great debt, for what he accomplished in the development of the mountain country as a summer resort and in the introduction of city conveniences, methods, and cuisine into hotel life in the hills.

The availability of a handful of large and tastefully appointed hotels in the White Mountains by the late 1840s signaled a transformation in the nature of tourism in America's "most accessible wilderness." This transformation culminated by mid-century in the coming of the railroad, an event that stimulated the region's economy by literally placing the noble landscapes of northern New England at the doorstep of an entire nation. Far superior in speed and comfort to the stagecoaches then in use, the iron horse would usher in a golden age in the White Mountains as it left the heroic era of rustic taverns and colorful mountain men far behind.

Successful farming in the highlands depended on the raising of a wide variety of crops and animals. Farmers also hunted in the fall, logged in the winter, and "sugared" in the spring.

6. The Golden Age

If the Willey Disaster of 1826 was the steering mechanism for the early White Mountain touring experience, the arrival of the railroad in 1851 was the "engine" that propelled the region's tourist industry toward its full potential. From their modest beginnings in the mid-1830s, railways quickly became the preferred method in this country for transporting passengers and freight over long distances. In the White Mountains and other east coast resort areas, the economic effects of the railroad's birth were nothing short of phenomenal. Not until the early twentieth century, with the dawning of the automobile age, were the railroads forced to relinquish their hold on the nation's transportation networks.

During the 1840s, a number of railways slowly made their way toward the White Mountains. The earlier transportation links forged between Boston and the mountains, recreated as rail lines, extended from that city to Portsmouth by 1840, and to Concord and Portland by 1842. Four years later, the first railroad to actually penetrate the White Mountains was organized in Portland by the "Father of Maine Railroads," John Alfred Poor.

Born in Andover, Maine, a picturesque farming community on the eastern fringe of the White Mountains, Poor had witnessed a steam locomotive haul the first train on the Boston and Worcester Railroad. Inspired by this thrilling event, he conceived a plan for a railroad connection between Portland and Montreal, which was then a natural reservoir for western grain products destined for Europe. By building this line, Poor hoped to stimulate commercial activity in his native state and to pull Portland out of an economic decline by turning it into an ice-free port for goods shipped from the Great Lakes through Montreal.

In January 1845, upon hearing that Boston interests were presenting their own case to the Montreal Board of Trade, Poor undertook an epic five-day trip through severe snowstorms to delay a vote. His eloquent and persuasive speech on the superiority of the Montreal-to-Portland route, combined with fears that Boston might attempt to dominate the Canadian port just as it had extended its control over Portland with the recently completed rail link to that city, convinced the Board of Trade to vote in Portland's favor.

In 1846, construction of the "Atlantic and St. Lawrence Railroad" was begun on the Portland waterfront, with much of the money coming from the Forest City

(Portland would eventually contribute over $3,000,000 through loans and stock subscriptions) as well as other financial backers. Construction moved along at a slow but steady pace during the next few years, with tracks reaching the "grand cathedral district" of the Androscoggin Valley at Bethel in March of 1851. Documenting the arrival of the railroad a few months later in Gorham, only eight miles north of Mount Washington, Dr. Nathaniel Tuckerman True wrote in his 1882 history of that town:

> Trains commenced to run regularly in July 1851. A large number of persons from the seacoast towns made an excursion to Gorham that year. The most of them had never been among the mountains, and their sudden transportation from a comparatively level to a mountainous country was a novel and exciting sensation.

Two years later, on July 18, 1853, regular service between Portland and Montreal commenced, with the line being leased to the Grand Trunk Railway of Canada for a term of 999 years. Thanks to this new technological wonder, visitors from such American urban centers as Boston, New York, Philadelphia, and Baltimore, as well as Canadian cities to the north, could now reach the White Mountains in a matter of hours instead of days.

The tremendous expansion of White Mountain tourism during the 1850s and 1860s was a clear result of railroad development, but it was not the only segment of the region's economy to benefit from this new mode of transport. Trains hauling

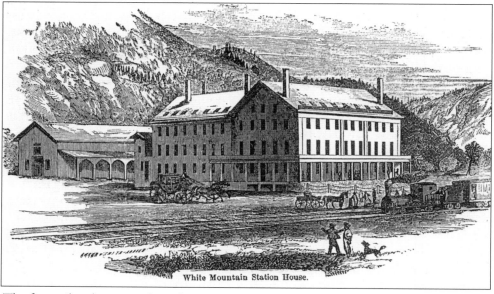

White Mountain Station House.

The first railroad to enter the White Mountains arrived in Gorham, New Hampshire, in 1851. The Alpine House or "White Mountain Station House" was among the earliest grand hotels in the region.

carloads of passengers into the northern highlands could just as easily convey locally grown produce and trees to outside markets. Consequently, freight yards, livestock pens, and storehouses began to crop up near railway depots. For those living in towns through which the railroad passed, the economic benefits must have seemed endless, and populations in some communities, including Gorham, as much as quadrupled over the next decade. Within a few years, however, North Country farmers found themselves competing with agricultural products shipped east from the expanding American West, and many therefore turned to the region's growing logging industry, which was less susceptible to such competition.

Despite these necessary adjustments, all along the Grand Trunk's New England route commercial ventures blossomed and the pace of industrialization quickened. In 1852, in direct response to the railroad's arrival, several wealthy Portland businessmen, including John Bundy Brown, J.S. Little, and Hezekiah Wilson, established lumber mills at Berlin Falls, just upriver from Gorham; thanks to the railroad and a vast source of raw material, this mill complex, later known as the Brown Company, would become by 1890 the largest producer of sawn lumber east of the Mississippi River. Before the 1870s, when the Grand Trunk's steam engines were converted from wood to coal burners, the forested hills of the Androscoggin Valley also provided an abundant supply of fuel for the smoke-belching locomotives.

Although the first railroad through the White Mountains (Canada's "Road to the Sea") was constructed primarily as a freight carrier, there are numerous indications that the railroad's backers recognized the potential for passenger traffic if the line was placed close to the "lofty crags and wildest steeps" of the Presidential Range. John Alfred Poor's original plan had taken the railroad's path through the "mournful grandeur" of Dixville Notch, some 50 miles to the north, but surveyors concluded that an expensive tunnel would have been required to get the tracks safely through that pass.

The most obvious sign of the railroad's interest in profiting from the tourist business was the construction from 1850 to 1851 of the 165-room White Mountain Station House, or first Alpine House, on the Gorham Common. Combining the facilities of a railway station with the refined elegance of a hotel, the Alpine House was completed just in time to receive guests from the railroad's inaugural run. The largest wooden structure in the entire town, the Alpine House displayed Italianate architectural features, including a broad, wrap-around porch on its main front, a design element that would become a staple in hotels built throughout the region. This impressive and well-appointed structure, which stood until 1872 and by some estimates cost the then princely sum of $30,000, was, along with the Conway House and first Crawford House, among the earliest grand resort hotels in the White Mountains. Beckett's *Guide Book of the Atlantic and St. Lawrence*, published in 1853, furnishes a glimpse of summer life at this hotel shortly after it opened:

> Here, perchance, you are greeted with the scenes which usually attend
> an arrival at a fashionable resort—ladies in their sun bonnets gliding to

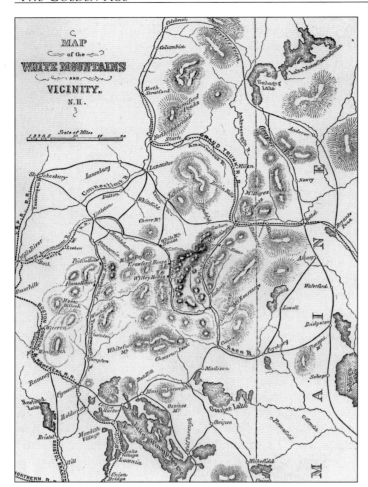

Railroads had reached the White Mountain towns of Gorham and Littleton when this late 1850s map was published. The coming of the railroads transformed the area's economy.

and fro, anxious to see the newcomers, gentlemen under curiously shaped hats and wreaths of cigar smoke, lounging prominently against pillar and post as anxious to show their indifference; hurrying waiters bumping trunks and boxes against the elbows of the promiscuous crowd in the hall, &c.

But barring contingencies, you are immediately shown to a neat and airy room, and having adjusted the outer man, the next thing is to look about the house. You will find it a noble edifice, three stories in height, and one hundred feet front by fifty in width, with an ell of about the same dimensions. A handsome piazza along the front and two ends, gives a finish to the building, while it affords a pleasant walk, where visitors may enjoy the mountain air and scenery.

Within, you find broad and lofty halls, and ample parlors, sitting and withdrawing rooms, fitted and furnished with corresponding elegance—a noble dining room, eighty feet by thirty, and sleeping rooms sufficient to accommodate two hundred and fifty persons.

By this time you probably begin to think of dinner, the sudden transition from the atmosphere of the ocean to the bracing air of the mountains being a keen whetter of the appetite. On this score, you could not submit your case to more considerate persons than the landlord and landlady, Mr. Hitchcock and Mrs. Hayes.

We are not sure but that the mass of travelers would respond to the exclamation of a fellow tourist, that about the pleasantest feature in a day's travel, is the dinner hour. And certainly to escape from the fervor of a July or August sun to tables nicely spread with every variety of viand that your nicest metropolitan hotel can boast, and some things that such cannot boast, the delicately flavored trout of the mountain rivulet for instance, is very apt to produce that complacent state of mind which disposes one to the enjoyment of the intellectual.

Dinner over, unless you prefer for company the fancies that hover around a cigar, in the smoking room, let's stroll under the portico. You find yourself in the centre of a broad level or table land, closed up by mountains on all sides, a wonderful depression through which the Androscoggin makes the passage of the hills, the foundations of the hotel being but 802 feet above tide water at Portland.

The availability of rail transportation to Gorham temporarily shifted the focus of White Mountain tourism to the east and away from the older tourist centers in Crawford and Franconia Notches. But the Atlantic and St. Lawrence Railroad was merely the first of several railroads to enter or approach the White Mountains in the late 1840s and early 1850s, and the owners of hotels and boarding houses without direct access to the railroad were quick to set up stage routes to whatever terminus was closest. Nonetheless, the Grand Trunk Railway's proximity to Mount Washington's summit gave it a clear advantage over competing lines until the 1870s, when tracks at last penetrated the heart of the mountains at Crawford Notch.

In 1848, the Northern Railroad was completed from Concord to White River Junction, Vermont, where it made a connection with the Connecticut and Passumpsic Rivers Railroad to Wells River, Vermont. From there, a stagecoach could transport people to the mountains in less than a day's time. By 1853, a third all-rail route developed making use of the Boston, Concord, and Montreal Railroad, which ran from Concord through Laconia and Plymouth to Woodsville, where passengers switched to the White Mountains Railroad for the final leg of the journey to Littleton.

In anticipation of the railroad's arrival in the western district of the mountains, Littleton storekeeper Henry L. Thayer constructed a three-and-a-half story hotel on the town's main street in 1850; with its splendid Greek Revival portico and rooftop cupola, Thayer's Hotel has miraculously survived to the present, giving it the distinction of being the oldest hotel structure of its type in the White

A party of Crawford House guests prepare to ascend Mount Washington on horseback via the Crawford Path. This trail was converted for use by saddle ponies in 1840.

Mountains. During the early 1850s, the convenience of the Boston, Concord, and Montreal route also gave tourists the option of leaving the trains at The Weirs, just north of Laconia, and then traveling across Lake Winnipesaukee on the steamboat *Lady of the Lake*, which had been launched in 1849. Upon reaching Center Harbor, travelers could then take the short stagecoach ride to Conway.

Having successfully operated a small inn at the northern gateway to Crawford Notch for some 20 years, and well aware of the boom in tourism that the fast-approaching railroads would bring forth, Thomas J. Crawford borrowed money in 1850 to start construction of a substantial hotel on a knoll west of his Notch House property. Crawford's ambitious scheme proved more expensive than originally thought, however, and following in the footsteps of his brother, Ethan Allen, he soon found himself over-extended financially. As a consequence, Crawford sold both the Notch House and the unfinished hotel late in 1850 to Ebenezer Eastman of Littleton, who completed construction by the spring of 1851 and hired Joseph L. Gibb as manager.

It was under the watchful eye of Gibb, who had launched his White Mountain hotel career at the Lafayette House in Franconia Notch, that this imposing 200-room structure achieved a high level of popularity. With its picturesque view of Saco Lake and the famous Gate of the Notch, the first Crawford House furnished an elegant retreat to thousands of tourists until it was regrettably destroyed by fire on April 3, 1859. Unwilling to forego that season's receipts, the hotel's owners, a group of men from Littleton and Haverhill, Massachusetts, moved quickly to rebuild, hauling lumber from Littleton and hiring 150 men and 75 oxen and horses to conduct the work. According to *The History of Coos County* (1888), another Crawford House, built on an even larger scale, stood on the old site just over 60 days after construction started, opening its doors to the public on July 13, 1859, "when 40 received dinner, and 100 were entertained for the night."

Erected in 1850 by partners Hiram Abbott, Samuel Thoms, and Nathaniel Abbott, and opened on July 1, 1851, the Conway House was a substantial Greek Revival-styled wooden hotel offering accommodations as sophisticated as those found at the Alpine House and Crawford House. Although nearby North Conway village, which would become a major hub of tourism in the 1860s, could claim a handful of modest hostelries by this time (Kearsarge Tavern, North Conway House), many well-to-do visitors preferred to stay at the stylish 100-room Conway House, especially since it functioned as a way-station for local stage lines managed by the hotel owners. Like the Alpine House and Crawford House, this imposing hotel occupied a conspicuous site, in this instance a corner lot at the junction of four heavily traveled roads in the center of Conway village. From 1851 to 1856, the Conway House was managed by Horace Fabyan, the famous White Mountain hotel man. Among its early guests were John Greenleaf Whittier, Franklin Pierce, and Horace Greeley.

Except for the Alpine House in Gorham and the second Pemigewasset House in Plymouth, the latter financed in 1863 by the Boston, Concord, and Montreal Railroad, most of the grand hotels of the White Mountains would be built and

The Conway House's stylish Greek Revival exterior was matched by equally sophisticated interior appointments. Among the hotel's early guests were John Greenleaf Whittier and Horace Greeley.

managed by "hotel companies" not railroad controlled. Nevertheless, from the outset of the so-called "Golden Age" of tourism in the early 1850s, railroads and hotels developed a unique, interdependent relationship based on close cooperation and mutual support. In order to fill their rooms and larders, the hotels needed the railroads to bring tourists and supplies to the mountains. The railroads, in turn, promoted the hotels as travel destinations by issuing guidebooks, maps, and illustrated pamphlets showing these self-contained "cities in the wilderness," as well as many of the scenic attractions in their vicinity. Once the railroads were in place, it was inevitable that the next step would be to construct even larger hotels, or expand existing ones, close to the region's chief attractions: the Old Man of the Mountain, the Flume, Crawford Notch, and, of course, Mount Washington. Since the Northeast's highest peak was only a few miles south of the Alpine House at Gorham, and it was the mountains' earliest railway "depot," the entrepreneurial fever struck there first.

During the spring of 1850, in anticipation of the great wave of well-heeled vacationers coming to the mountains through Gorham, the Atlantic and St. Lawrence Railroad assigned a gang of workmen the job of laying out a road connecting Gorham with the highway through Pinkham Notch, which then ran from the town of Randolph to Jackson. Now part of Route 16, the "Glen Road" joined up with the old thoroughfare just below the farm of Hayes and Dolly Copp. By the summer of the following year, stagecoaches were making daily runs between Gorham and Conway, with guests at the Alpine House traveling by stage in about an hour directly to the base of Mount Washington. Once there, they could climb some 4,600 feet to the very top of New England by way of a seven-mile "horse road," later known as the Glen House Bridle Path. Not surprisingly, construction of this winding trail was also financed by the Atlantic and St. Lawrence Railroad as one more way of attracting customers to the mid-point of its Portland-to-Montreal route.

Perhaps the most famous of the earliest grand hotels in the White Mountains was the first Glen House, located 8 miles south of Gorham on the east side of the Pinkham Notch road. It had its beginnings in a modest "public house" erected in the late 1840s by John Bellows, an Exeter land speculator. In 1850 and 1851, "a few guests were entertained" here, but in the spring of 1852 Bellows made a quick profit by selling his inn and 700 acres of land to "Colonel" Joseph M. Thompson, a native of the nearby town of Shelburne and former proprietor of the Casco Bay House in Portland. Thompson "had much of the showman in his make-up," stated F. Allen Burt in his authoritative work, *The Story of Mount Washington* (1960), and he immediately hired carpenters to finish a small annex that had been started by Bellows. As a result, during the 1852 season, landlord Thompson could offer some two dozen guest rooms to patrons of the "Glen House," as he now called the place.

Thanks to Thompson's genial nature and able management—and his wife's good cooking—the Glen House became increasingly popular with tourists, and by the fall of 1852 it was apparent that additional guest accommodations were needed. Construction work was begun at once, and by the season of 1853 an

The most famous of the early White Mountain grand hotels was the Glen House in Pinkham Notch. The hotel was doubled in size in 1866 and burned in 1884.

elegant three-and-a-half story hotel stood on the site of the old Bellows inn. In its original form, the Glen House was 120 feet long and 44 feet wide. In 1866, with a carriage road on Mount Washington drawing hundreds of new visitors to the Glen, Thompson decided to more than double the size of the hotel. Boasting numerous guest amenities, the expanded Glen House came to be regarded as the ultimate in hotel accommodations in the eastern district of the White Mountains.

The 1867 edition of Samuel C. Eastman's *White Mountain Guide Book* provides an interesting portrait of the first Glen House, which by then had nearly 200 rooms and a parlor purported to be the largest in any American hotel:

> The Glen House has been enlarged the past season, so that it is now one of the largest and grandest hotels of the White Mountain region. In fact, a new hotel, equal in size to the one that formerly occupied the spot, has been built and attached to the old house. The office and receiving hall occupy a spacious apartment between the old and the new. The parlor is a magnificent room, 100 by 50 feet, elegantly furnished. The dining room is a fine hall, in which all the 600 guests, which the hotel will now easily accommodate, may dine at once without trouble or

inconvenience. From the balcony of the hotel may be had an uninterrupted view of the highest summits in New England, while the parties ascending and descending the rugged ledges of Mt. Washington may be watched by the aid of a glass. The whole front of the house, facing the mountains and the rushing Peabody River, contains rooms that are unusually attractive, while those on the other side are also favored with remarkable and pleasing mountain views.

As luxurious as Joseph Thompson's Glen House may have been in its heyday, his extraordinary success as a hotel-keeper had even more to do with the types of activities offered to his visitors. In this regard, Thompson seems to have been especially resourceful. Besides short walks and "rambles" about the hotel grounds, guests at the Glen House could ascend to "Prospect Rock" for a view of the Carter-Moriah Range looming across the valley behind the hotel. For those desiring longer walks or a short carriage ride, the "Avenue of Cascades," a four-mile stretch of road leading toward Jackson, offered an impressive series of waterfalls and gorges, including the famed Emerald Pool. Other sites in Pinkham Notch much favored by Glen House guests were Thompson's Falls, the Crystal Cascade, Glen Ellis Falls (renamed from "Pitcher Falls" by Thompson in 1852), and Tuckerman Ravine. For those with greater fortitude, there was always the trip up Mount Washington on the Glen House Bridle Path. The temptation to ascend it upon first arriving at the hotel was something the proprietor discouraged, for an early edition of *The Glen House Book* states, "Most people prefer to hold that excursion in reserve, wisely we think, because it is apt to dwarf everything else by comparison. Besides, the mountain excursion, to do it justice, ought only to be undertaken on clear, or comparatively clear days, of which there are by no means too many in the course of a season."

TOP - OF Mᵗ WASHINGTON 6295 FEET ABOVE THE LEVEL OF THE SEA.
Entered according to Act of Congress, in the year 1855, by John H. Spaulding, in the Clerk's office of the District Court of the District of Massachusetts.

By 1853, Mount Washington's peak boasted two stone shelters securely anchored by cables. The "observatory" between the buildings had a platform that, when raised, allowed visitors a better view.

Since many well off tourists remained at the grand hotels for several weeks at a time, additional diversions were necessary. At the Glen House, visitors enjoyed such recreational and cultural activities as croquet, tennis, horseback riding, card parties, billiards, dances, lectures, and plays. And, of course, there was the food, which was as rich and varied as one would find in any city hotel in America or Europe. On the nearby "hotel farm," a herd of cows provided guests with fresh milk, cream, and butter. Most of the hotel's vegetables were grown here as well. Finally, so that friends at home could share in all of these delights, the Glen House contained its own post office and the latest in telegraph equipment.

The coming of the railroad to Gorham and the opening of the Glen House brought forth an increased demand for a permanent, overnight facility on the summit of Mount Washington. Requests for such a shelter were also heard from tourists ascending from the western side. "In conception and execution, the task was a truly herculean one," stated a contemporary guidebook, but Joseph S. Hall and Lucius M. Rosebrook of Lancaster, and Nathan R. Perkins of Jefferson "were found equal to it."

On June 1, 1852, these men began blasting stone for the walls of Mount Washington's first "Summit House," and within days the top of Trinity Height was a flurry of activity. All of the lumber for the sheathing and roof was sawn out at a mill in Jefferson and carried up the Stillings Path, which started in Jefferson Highlands and extended for nine miles to a point near the Castellated Ridge, whence Mount Washington could be reached over the slopes of Mounts Jefferson and Clay. "A chain was hung over the horse's back and one end of each board was run through a loop at the end of the chain, two boards being carried on each side of the horse," wrote the White Mountain historian Frederick W. Kilbourne. "The drivers, D. S. Davis and A. Judson Bedell, walked behind carrying the farther end of the boards." Tradition has it that Lucius Rosebrook carried the heavy front door up on his back, with a jug of molasses in his hand "for good measure." This rude but welcoming shelter opened to the public on July 28, 1852, serving meals to 53 guests and hosting 12 for the night. To safeguard the building against destruction from high winds, four "stout cables" two inches thick were passed over the roof and securely fastened to large iron bolts cemented into the summit rocks.

So successful was Mount Washington's new Summit House that the following year the famous Tip-Top House, a nearly identical stone shelter, was erected nearby. Recently restored to something resembling its original appearance, and now the oldest structure remaining on the summit, Tip-Top's massive six-foot stone walls and nearly flat deck roof were erected in 1853 by a rival firm led by Samuel Fitch Spaulding of Lancaster and his nephew, John Hubbard Spaulding, author of the popular mid-nineteenth century guidebook, *Historical Relics of the White Mountains* (1855).

Like the Summit House, Tip-Top contained a dining hall, a small kitchen, and a row of sleeping "berths" filled with moss and separated from the rest of the room by partitions covered in a heavy cotton cloth. During the first season both

Before the opening of the Mount Washington Carriage Road and Cog Railway, bridle paths gave visitors access to the summit, as illustrated in this sketch by Winslow Homer.

hostelries were open, competition was keen, but in 1854 the Spauldings gained control of both houses. With its rooftop telescope and tiny bar sporting a pot-bellied stove and shelves "filled with decanters," the Tip-Top House displayed a picturesque charm that appealed to residents of the grand hotels far below.

The inn's allure helped offset its somewhat restricted menu, which consisted mainly of bacon, ham, tripe, tongue, eggs, pancakes, fried cakes, and a variety of hot breads and biscuits. From 1862 to 1872, when a much larger Summit House was built, both buildings were leased to Colonel John R. Hitchcock, proprietor of the Alpine House in Gorham. In 1853 and 1861, the low deck roofs on the Summit House and Tip-Top House, respectively, were replaced with steeply-pitched roofs allowing for a second story containing tiny sleeping rooms. Among the better known guests who stayed in these two stone shelters were Charles Sumner, Horace Greeley, William H. Seward, and Jefferson Davis. The first Summit House was demolished in 1884.

No discussion of the earliest group of grand hotels in the White Mountains would be complete without mentioning the first Profile House, which occupied an outstanding location at the northern entrance to Franconia Notch from 1852 to 1905. Early in the former year, partners Richard Taft, George T. Brown, and Ira Coffin, working under the name of "Flume and Franconia Hotel Company," acquired the Lafayette House and a sizable tract of land lying between Profile and Echo Lakes. These enterprising businessmen then directed the creation of a massive wooden hotel whose porticoed entrance faced onto a stunning view of nearby Eagle Cliff, Profile Lake, and the lower ramparts of Mount Lafayette. Looking very much like the oldest section of the Glen House, the three-and-a-half story, 110-room Profile House was ready for occupancy in July of 1853. During the hotel's construction, the old Lafayette House was moved across the road to a spot behind it, where it was converted into dormitory housing for the Profile House staff.

Paralleling the resort hotel development in Pinkham Notch to the east, the opening of the Profile House was gauged to coincide with the arrival of passenger trains into Littleton in 1853; the burgeoning transportation system thus made it possible for the urban elite to reach the hotel entirely by rail, apart from a brief stage journey of about an hour. In 1866, Colonel Charles H. Greenleaf joined the firm, and two major additions to the hotel were thereafter carried out, eventually enabling some 500 guests to be lodged at the same time. Further expansion at the Profile House began in 1868, when the first of some twenty stylish summer "cottages" were erected on the hotel grounds as part of this fashionable playground in the wilds.

Other White Mountain hotel complexes, including the Waumbek at Jefferson, the Wentworth Hall and Cottages at Jackson, and the Waterville Inn and Cottages at Waterville Valley, would follow a similar pattern of providing more "private" accommodations for well-to-do guests who wished to exercise their need for exclusivity. Indulging their affluent clientele even further, the Profile House's owners completed a 9-mile narrow gauge railroad between Bethlehem Junction and the hotel in 1879, eliminating the need for the stage ride from Littleton. In addition to the amenities already mentioned in connection with the Glen House, the Profile House offered its guests such enticements as bowling alleys, a music room, boat excursions on Echo and Profile Lakes, and guided tours to such local attractions as the Flume, the Pool, the Basin, and the Old Man of the Mountain.

In the same year that the Profile House opened its doors, the artist Benjamin Champney purchased a house in North Conway where he set up a studio. Champney's decision to locate in a "suburb of Paradise" was based partly on a growing interest among American artists, especially those from the so-called Hudson River School, in the sublime beauty of the White Mountains. It was also grounded in the realities of consumerism, for no self-respecting tourist of means could return home without purchasing a painting of the breathtaking mountain scenery. In his autobiography, *Sixty Years' Memories of Art and Artists* (1900), Champney recalled his initial satisfaction with the North Conway area:

> We were delighted with the surrounding scenery, the wide stretch of the intervales, broken with well-tilled farms, the fields just ripening for the harvest, with the noble elms dotted about in pretty groups. Then beyond the Saco, the massive forms of the ledges rose up, their granite walls covered with forests. But behind these and above all was the broken line of Moat Mt.
>
> To the north Mt. Washington and its attendant peaks bounded the view. Then came Kearsarge on the right, and the lesser Rattlesnake range

on the east. The whole formed a scene of surpassing beauty, rarely to be found anywhere. We had seen grander, higher mountains in Switzerland, but not often so much beauty and artistic picturesqueness brought together in one valley.

. . . In 1852, after a detour to Moosehead Lake, I came once more to North Conway with Hamilton Wilde, who had just returned from his studies in Europe. There was quite a little knot of artists at Thompson's, and we nearly filled the dining table in the old house. A few devoted lovers of North Conway were in this little village occupying the two or three houses where guests were taken in. Thus every year brought fresh visitors to North Conway as the news of its attractions spread, until in 1853 and 1854 the meadows and the banks of the Saco were dotted all about with white umbrellas in great numbers. The fine old boulders, fallen from the Cathedral Ledge, mossy and gray, were very attractive to the student. The Intervale at Lower Bartlett drew us often to that part of the valley. Coleman, Hubbard, Gifford and Shattuck of New York, settled themselves at the old farmhouse, now remodelled and occupied by Mr. George Wolcott near the Mt. Moat House.

Like Benjamin Champney, his friend John Frederick Kensett became fascinated with the majestic scenery of the White Mountains at mid-century, having made his first visit to the region in the fall of 1849. A year later, in company with Champney and artist John Casilear, he returned to North Conway to make sketches of the surrounding landscape. In the winter of the same year in his New York studio, Kensett painted *Mount Washington from the Valley of Conway*, a panoramic view masterfully conveying a sense of harmony between man and nature. Critics bestowed high praise when it was exhibited, and in 1851 the American Art-Union issued 13,500 copies of the work in the form of an engraving by James Smillie. Widely circulated among artists and their patrons, this popular print, and the view that inspired it, came to represent the vanishing American wilderness to a public caught up in a world of increasing industrialization.

Within the next two decades, a handful of artist colonies would spring up among the mountains, most notably in Jackson, West Campton, and, of course, North Conway. Because they painted the same subject matter and based their work on similar aesthetic ideals, these artists have been referred to as members of the "White Mountain School." Although their primary studios were often located beyond the confines of the White Mountains, it was in connection with the grand hotels in the region where such talented artists and their work came to be known. In time, the "artist-in-residence" would be regarded by American and European travelers as a significant component of the summer resort experience. Since these artists also functioned as special hotel guests by hosting social functions and organizing cultural events, their work remained popular well after photographs of the region became commercially available.

The first Profile House stood at the northern entrance to Franconia Notch from 1852 to 1905. Its opening coincided with the railroad's arrival in nearby Littleton.

The list of important American and European artists who painted in the mountains during the second half of the nineteenth century, or established studios in the grand hotels during this same time, is a lengthy one, but among the most prominent were Frank H. Shapleigh, Albert Bierstadt, Edward Hill, Asher Brown Durand, Benjamin Bellows Grant Stone, William Morris Hunt, Thomas Hill, Samuel Griggs, George Inness, John Joseph Enneking, and Godfrey Nicholas Frankenstein. The German-born Frankenstein first visited the Crawford Notch area in 1847, returning later to sketch in the vicinity and stay with the reclusive Boston dentist Dr. Samuel Bemis at his stone manor house, now called Notchland Inn. This artist's name is commemorated in the steep cliffs that rise up at the southern end of the notch, and in "Frankenstein Trestle," a 500-foot steel span erected below the precipitous bluff in 1875.

Because of their size, opulence, and services, places like the Glen House, Crawford House, Alpine House, Conway House, and Profile House created an atmosphere in the 1850s wherein the grand hotel experience was viewed as synonymous with the "White Mountain tour." As the tourist industry expanded during that decade and the American economy became more dependent on mass-consumerism, a modified version of that "tour" became available to a more diverse range of people, including successful merchants, laborers, and even farmers.

With their widely varying backgrounds, these new tourists usually spent less time in the mountains than their well-to-do counterparts, and therefore wished to be directed to the area's most interesting attractions as quickly as possible. Hence, such tourists welcomed the many guidebooks then being published, including some that went so far as to recommend the correct way of appreciating

97

the local scenery. Since many tourists of the "Golden Age" regarded traveling to the White Mountains as a form of high culture, such publications, especially those that interpreted the landscape in a romantic vein, were extremely popular. Of the early guidebooks composed in this manner, one written by the Reverend Thomas Starr King was by far considered the best.

King, an eloquent Unitarian pastor of the Hollis Street Society of Boston, first visited the White Mountains in July 1849 when he was 25 years of age. A passionate lover of all that was grand and beautiful in nature, King, along with a few friends, took the usual route of the pre-railroad days on this trip, "traveling in an overloaded stage to Conway." The next day they made their way to Crawford Notch, and when they "were standing directly in front of the Willey House, a heavy peal of thunder and the associations and scenes of the place profoundly moved them," King later recorded.

So enthusiastic was King about the White Hills that he returned to the region many times, most often making Gorham his headquarters. In 1853, he began to print accounts of his explorations among the mountains in the pages of the *Boston Transcript*. These columns, with their rich descriptions and lengthy quotations from the work of the romantic poets, were compiled and published in book form in 1859 under the title *The White Hills: Their Legends, Landscape, and Poetry*. Over 400 pages long, King's "guidebook" contained historical and scientific information contributed by Reverend Benjamin G. Willey and Professor Edward Tuckerman, and was embellished with numerous engravings of the sublime scenery in the region.

Known as the "Man at the Pool," John Merrill was a notable White Mountain character. From 1853 to about 1887 he entertained Franconia Notch visitors with his homespun philosophy.

King's great love for the White Mountains is most evident in his descriptions of the Androscoggin River Valley near Gorham. Noting the railroad platform at the Alpine House was not situated where the mountains could be seen at their best vantage, he nevertheless believed that "as a general thing, Gorham is the place to see the more rugged sculpturing and the Titanic brawn of the hills." He continued:

> Turning from North Conway to the Androscoggin Valley is somewhat like turning from a volume of Tennyson to the pages of Carlyle; from the melodies of Don Giovanni to the surges of the Ninth Symphony; from the art of Raffaello to that of Michel Angelo.

King avoided such flowery language, however, when admonishing his readers to take their time when experiencing the numerous "treasures of ever changing beauty" in the district:

> Some travelers have but a very few days for the whole tour of the mountain region, and desire, in that time, to see the points of interest that are the most striking, and that will produce the strongest sensation. These will hurry at once by stage to "The Glen," after their days ride in the [railroad] cars, that they may reach as quickly as possible the very base of Mount Washington. Their object will then be to make the ascent of it at once, and hurry around to "The Notch," which is thirty-six miles from "The Glen," requiring nine or ten hours by stage. . . . The difficulty is, that in rushing so fast as many of us do through the mountains, the mountains do not have time to come to us. . . . If we could learn, or be content, to use a week at some central point of any valley, instead of hurrying through all of them—to spend the same money at one spot that is usually spread over the lengthened journey—to take the proper times for driving quietly to the best positions—we should see vastly more, as any of the intelligent visitors in North Conway will assure us. We should understand not only topography, but scenery.

In a chapter of *The White Hills* entitled "The Ascent of Mount Washington," Reverend King advocated the eastern approach for those wanting to climb the great mountain, a primary goal of most White Mountain sojourners. "The Glen route is the shortest," he proclaimed, not surprisingly. Regarding the actual ascent from the Pinkham Notch side, he wrote, "For the first four miles the horses keep the wide and hard track, with a regular ascent of one foot in eight, which was laid out for a carriage road to the summit, but never completed." This remark obviously appeared in one of King's *Boston Transcript* columns published soon after the abandonment in late 1856 of the wagon road up Mount Washington. Had King not departed for California about the time his White Mountain guidebook was published three years later, he might have rejoiced, with others, in the completion of what John H. Spaulding termed "a carriage-route that for novelty,

White Mountain landscapes have inspired countless works of art over the years. The firm of Currier and Ives issued this view of Mount Washington and the Presidential Range from Conway in 1860.

and unparalleled wonder-exciting location, will not in the western world have an equal." Finally reaching the top of the monarch of New England in 1861, the Mount Washington Carriage (now "Auto") Road has been called "the world's first mountain toll road, and America's oldest man-made tourist attraction."

The history of "The Road to the Sky" began in 1853, the same year the Tip-Top House opened to the public and the last spike was driven on the railroad between Portland and Montreal. In July, the state legislature approved a charter with a capital of $50,000 for the "Mount Washington Road Company," the brainchild of General David O. Macomber of Middletown, Connecticut. A few weeks later, on September 1, the company was organized at a meeting held in the parlor of the Alpine House in Gorham. Macomber, who was voted president, had conceived the idea of building a macadamized road 16 feet wide up the eastern side of the great mountain. In potentially unsafe locations, he proposed that stone walls three feet high be erected, and on the very pinnacle he planned to construct an enormous masonry hotel with a rooftop observatory.

To raise money for this ambitious project, the company authorized three Portland men, Abner Lowell, Robert Robinson, and William Senter, to sell stock certificates. Based on their initial success, a survey for the eight-mile carriage road that took the most picturesque route was carried out, as was a revised determination of the mountain's height at 6,284 feet, 4 feet under the presently accepted elevation and 4 feet over the height measured by Captain Thomas Jefferson Cram of the United States Coast Survey in 1852–1853.

Construction of the Mount Washington Carriage Road began in 1855 under a contract awarded at $8,000 per mile. Utilizing horses, oxen, and large quantities of black powder, a crew of as many as 80 laborers slowly worked their way along, removing great quantities of trees and ledge as they progressed up the behemoth's steep side. In the meantime, the Abbot-Downing Company of Concord, makers of the famous Concord coach, had received an order from General Macomber to start work on a dozen specially-designed omnibuses equipped with powerful brakes and pairs of large screws in the floor that could be used to keep the vehicles level when going up or down the mountain.

By the fall of 1856, the first four miles of the road had been completed to a huge ledge known as "The Horn," and a modest shelter for the workers, the "Halfway House," had been built. However, there the work stopped for lack of funds. Unable to find new backers to cover the considerable cost still remaining, General Macomber "left the mountains, never to return." For the next three years, the carriage road project languished, but in 1859, thanks to the financial aid of David Pingree of Salem, Massachusetts, a new company was formed and work resumed. Under the "Mount Washington Summit Road Company," the road was at last completed on August 8, 1861.

In order to beat out his rival and landlord of the Alpine House, John R. Hitchcock, Colonel Thompson of the Glen House drove a light carriage up three weeks before the official opening and, with some assistance in keeping the carriage upright, managed to traverse the last half mile atop the boulder-strewn Glen House Bridle Path, the road not then being completed. The opening of the Mount Washington Carriage Road was heralded throughout the country as a triumph of engineering skill.

Of the first group of tourists to make use of the new carriage road up Mount Washington, one of the most famous was Louisa May Alcott, who spent part of her summer vacation in 1861 at the nearby Alpine House. Alcott, who would achieve phenomenal success with her 1869 novel *Little Women*, recorded her impressions of the four-hour trip up the road in a mountain wagon "drawn by six buckskin-colored horses." She was fascinated by the weathered scrub at the treeline, the sheer drops, and the view through the telescope mounted on the roof of the Tip-Top House. Although she made no mention of it, Alcott doubtless noticed a conspicuous heap of rocks some 200 yards northeast of the summit marking the place where Mount Washington's most famous "victim" met her demise just a few years before. While ascending the mountain in September 1855 with her uncle and his daughter, 20-year-old Lizzie Bourne had "perished" from exhaustion and a slight heart defect when only a short distance from the summit buildings. Accounts of her death, the second on the mountain, appeared in many newspapers and guidebooks, captivating a public who viewed this morbid event as one more reason to make a pilgrimage to the very "Crown of New England." So his readers could fully appreciate the drama of this event and other recent misadventures on the mountain, Samuel C. Eastman included the following text in the 1867 edition of his *White Mountain Guide Book*:

> During the last part of the ascent one will see the pile of stones that marks the spot where Miss Bourne, of Kennebunk, Me., died, near midnight, in September, 1855, and where her uncle and cousin kept sad watch till dawn. They started in the afternoon, without a guide, to walk to the summit. Night and fog overtook them, and the young lady perished in the chill and darkness among the rocks, but a few rods from the house they were in search of. Quite near, also, is the shelving rock, beneath which the remains of an elderly gentleman from Wilmington, Del., were found in July, 1857. He had attempted to ascend the mountain alone, one afternoon in August of the year before, and must have been overtaken by storm, and cold, and darkness, near the summit. His watch, and some bank bills in his vest pocket, were found uninjured, though most of the body, and even part of the skeleton, were gone. A little further below, and at the left of the ascending path, the ledge is visible where Dr. Benjamin Ball, of Boston, passed two nights in the snow and sleet of an October storm, alone, without food or

Completed in 1861, the Mount Washington Auto Road is "America's oldest man-made tourist attraction." Heavy snows can delay the spring opening of the road, as suggested by this photo of June 28, 1926.

covering. He was rescued when nature was about sinking. His feet were frozen, and he could not speak. How his life was preserved in such exposure is a marvel. It is equally remarkable that, though his feet were severely frozen, they were saved.

Unlike Lizzie Bourne and many later visitors who would challenge Mount Washington's harsh environment and lose their lives, Dr. Benjamin L. Ball not only survived three days and two nights exposed to the "blasts and snows" above treeline, but was able to communicate his nerve-wracking experience in a fascinating 70-page book entitled *Three Days on the White Mountains: Being the Perilous Adventure of Dr. B.L. Ball on Mount Washington During October 25, 26, and 27, 1855*. The oft retold story of Dr. Ball's ordeal of 60 hours "without food, shelter or fire, with snow and ice only for drink" still has the ability to leave its listeners spellbound. Armed with only an overcoat, a cloth cap, an umbrella, and a stubborn determination to reach the top, the doctor confronted unfamiliar topography and extremely hostile weather amid the heights, and, in the process, became a cherished figure in North American mountaineering lore.

The beginning of the Civil War interrupted the lives of many year-round residents in the White Mountain region, but its effect on the flourishing tourist industry was marginal. This circumstance was indeed fortunate, for the local economy was becoming less and less dependent on agricultural production as many hill farms were abandoned and second generation farmers moved to more urban locations for jobs. Widespread industrial development in this country from the 1860s through the 1890s also generated higher incomes for the growing middle class, so more people enjoyed improved living conditions and had leisure time to spend in the mountains. Swelling demand for summer accommodations in the White Mountains brought on another burst of hotel development, resulting in larger and more opulent facilities serviced by an expanding network of railroads.

During the 1860s, a number of new hotels appeared in tourist towns throughout the White Mountains, and several older establishments were expanded or otherwise updated. In 1861, near the center of picturesque North Conway, the Kearsarge House was opened by Samuel Thompson, a close friend of the artist Benjamin Champney. Thompson's hotel, which stood on the south side of the village common, originally consisted of the old "Kearsarge Tavern," to which had been added a three-and-a-half story wing. Responding to the arrival in North Conway of the Portland and Ogdensburg Railroad (later the Maine Central) in August 1871, and the Eastern Railroad (later the Boston and Maine) in June 1872, Thompson greatly enlarged his hotel again, so that it ultimately housed up to 300 guests. With its gas-lighted rooms, tastefully decorated interior, and six-story tower, the Kearsarge House was considered the epitome of Victorian hotel-keeping in the White Mountains upon completion.

While the railroad's arrival was cause enough for Samuel Thompson's expansion of the Kearsarge House, a healthy competition among White Mountain hotel owners arose during this period, stimulating an already active construction

KEARSARGE HOUSE,

NORTH CONWAY, N. H.

S. W. & S. D. THOMPSON, Managers.

The Kearsarge is a first-class hotel in every respect. To those familiar with North Conway and its surroundings nothing need be said; but to those who are not, we will say that there is no place about the mountains that surpasses it for beauty of scenery and attractive points of interest, it being a very desirable point for a long or short sojourn. The views from the parlors and verandas of the Kearsarge are not to be surpassed, if equalled, by any house in or around the White Mountains; and as a place for persons troubled with lung or throat diseases and rheumatism, it has no equal as a favorite stopping place.

Favorable arrangements with permanent boarders will be made. No pains will be spared to make it one of the most attractive of summer resorts. Prices for board at the Kearsarge House have been much reduced, both for transient and permanent guests. Transient rates will be $3 per day. By the week, $10.50 to $17.50, according to location of rooms. For further particulars address as above.

North Conway's Kearsarge House was considered the epitome of White Mountain hotel-keeping when it opened in 1861. Mary Todd Lincoln, among other notables, once stayed here.

boom. Thus, it is not surprising that around 1868, a rival hotel to Thompson's establishment was built a few miles north at Intervale village, on a site affording one of the most superlative views of the Presidential Range found anywhere. A local landmark until 1923, when it was destroyed by fire, the Intervale House displayed some of the same architectural features as the Kearsarge and could accommodate roughly the same number of visitors. Although not as large as the Kearsarge or Intervale Houses, the Sunset Pavilion was opened in 1867 on North Conway's main street, a short distance north of the Kearsarge. A plain barn-like structure that survived until 1940, the Sunset had space for some 150 guests. Thanks to these tourist facilities, and a cluster of smaller boarding houses and guest cottages, one guidebook writer could exclaim of North Conway by the 1880s, "no rural resort in New England has such devoted partisans and ardent admirers, no village in the mountain region has refreshed and renewed so many thousands of weary citizens."

On the opposite side of the Presidential Range, and, like North Conway and Intervale, offering some of the most widely acclaimed scenery in the White Mountains, was the town of Jefferson. A favorite haunt of the Reverend Thomas Starr King, Jefferson began to take on the character of a true summer resort in 1860, when Benjamin Plaisted built the earliest portion of what would later become a sprawling hotel complex known as "The Waumbek House and Cottages." Within a few years of the Waumbek's opening, several smaller hotels were established in Jefferson, among them the Grand View House, the Jefferson Hill House, the Mount Adams House, and the Starr King House.

Further to the east and just into Maine, the town of Bethel was also blossoming as a place of resort for tourists. In his celebrated 1859 guidebook *The White Hills*, King referred to this mountainous community as the "North Conway of the eastern slope," pointing out that the views of the northern Presidential Range and Mount Moriah were particularly enchanting from this vantage point. By 1863, three large hotels with a combined capacity of some 200 guests had opened at the "dignified and well-to-do old village" of Bethel Hill in response to a steady influx of summer visitors to that scenic locale on the Grand Trunk Railway. A decade later, the arrival of the Portland and Ogdensburg Railroad in Fryeburg, Maine, spurred Asa O. Pike to enlarge and refurbish the Oxford House, which had been operated as a tavern a half century earlier by Pike's grandfather, Major Samuel Osgood. Like other White Mountain towns catering to tourists at this time, Fryeburg also provided travelers with a selection of more modest accommodations, including the Walker House and Elm Farm, which could house some 30 guests each.

The town of Jackson was late coming into its own as a summer resort, but thanks to how popular the local scenery was with certain White Mountain artists, its first hotel, the Jackson Falls House, began taking in guests in 1858. By the end of the following decade, several similar establishments had thrown open their doors, including the Iron Mountain House, the Glen Ellis House, and the Thorn Mountain House, the latter of which was absorbed into the Wentworth Hall hotel complex in the early 1880s.

Further to the west, in the small village of Twin Mountain in the town of Carroll, several miles north of Bretton Woods, brothers Asa T. and Oscar F. Barron of Quechee, Vermont, purchased an old farmhouse in 1867 that was located near the junction of roads leading to Jefferson, Bethlehem, Franconia, and Crawford Notch. In spring of the next year, the Barrons erected a two-and-a-half story L-shaped hotel they appropriately called the Twin Mountain House. An early guest was the famous theologian Henry Ward Beecher, who suffered greatly from hay fever and in visiting the White Mountains "happily found exemption there from the attacks of the disease." Over a period of 17 years, beginning in 1872, Beecher and his sister Harriet Beecher Stowe (author of the influential 1852 novel *Uncle Tom's Cabin*) made this their summer retreat. The famous minister's fiery Sunday sermons became so popular that a tent was set up next to the hotel to hold the crowds.

Of the many White Mountain communities benefiting from the expanding tourist trade in the 1860s, the town of Bethlehem stands out among the rest, as its

The Twin Mountain House was one of several grand hotels in and around Bretton Woods operated at one time by the Barron, Merrill, and Barron Company. Henry Ward Beecher spent many summers here.

healthful climate and superb mountain views were quite literally made known to the outside world "by accident." In 1863, while returning from an excursion to the top of nearby Mount Agassiz, the Honorable Henry Howard, later governor of Rhode Island, was injured when the coach he was riding in overturned. Howard spent the next few weeks convalescing in a "well-kept stage tavern" built in 1857 by John Sinclair on Bethlehem's main thoroughfare, and it was during that time when he became convinced of Bethlehem's potential as a summer resort. In fact, he was so impressed with the attractiveness of this upland location that he made extensive purchases of land, selling building lots on credit and lending money "to those who were disposed to go into the summer-hotel business." As it turned out Howard's enthusiasm for Bethlehem proved contagious, for within a few decades more than 30 hotels and boarding houses were functioning there, including the much-expanded "Sinclair House" that attained grand hotel status by the late 1870s. By this time, also, the railroad had reached Bethlehem from Littleton, and during the height of the summer season as many as ten trains a day brought tourists into town. For many years, Bethlehem served as the headquarters of the American Hay-Fever Association, its elevated location and pollen-free air providing speedy relief to hay-fever sufferers who numbered among their ranks a sizable Jewish population from New York and other east coast cities.

If Bethlehem's earliest tourists marveled over the extraordinary view of the Presidential Range from that "airy village," they must have been especially intrigued when, in the mid-1860s, a wide break in the forests began to advance slowly up a western ridge of Mount Washington. Presumably, every hotel-keeper in the mountains already knew the reason why crews of workmen were attacking the wilderness along a route following the bridle path opened by Ethan Allen Crawford in 1821. But even in an age of wondrous inventions and amazing technological progress, the explanation for all this activity seemed utterly fantastic: a railroad was being built to the top of New England's highest peak.

Railroads had been functioning in the United States for less than 30 years when, in 1858, Sylvester Marsh petitioned the state legislature for a charter to construct a cog railway to the summit of Mount Washington. Legend has it that one legislator was so amused by this proposal, he offered an amendment allowing Marsh to "build a railroad to the moon." Undaunted by such criticism, Marsh would go down in history as the genius behind the world's first mountain climbing railway, now a National Historic Civil and Mechanical Engineering Landmark.

Born in Campton in the upper Pemigewasset Valley in 1803, Sylvester Marsh left his native state at the age of 19 and eventually settled in Chicago, where he made his fortune in meat packing and grain drying enterprises. In 1855, having received 11 U.S. patents for inventions associated with his Chicago business ventures, he retired to the Jamaica Plain section of West Roxbury, Massachusetts. But the sedate life was not for Marsh, whose restless nature and inventive mind caused him to search for a new project. In August 1857, in company with the Boston theologian Augustus Thompson, Marsh went for a "tramp" in the White Mountains. While hiking up the

A mountain brake prepares to leave the Uplands hotel at Bethlehem, New Hampshire. By the 1920s, more than 30 summer hotels existed in this town.

107

Dating from the 1870s, Bethlehem's Maplewood Hotel was one of the most extensive resort complexes ever developed in the White Mountains. Only the Casino, on the right, and a few cottages remain.

Crawford Path, the two men were overtaken by a ferocious storm, and after stumbling along in freezing rain and high winds, they at last reached the safety of the Tip-Top House. As warmth returned to his frozen limbs, Marsh resolved to find a safer and easier way of ascending the formidable mountain.

From an early age, Marsh had been fascinated by steam railroad technology, and he now set to work designing a locomotive that could safely climb the very steep grades it would encounter on Mount Washington. In 1861, a patent was granted to him for an "Inclined Railroad," which featured a small, but powerful engine with a central cogwheel. A patent for a braking system using compressed air followed in 1864. With his own resources, Marsh purchased thousands of acres in the Ammonoosuc Valley, laid out a 6-mile access road to the western base of the mountain, surveyed a route to the top, and arranged for the construction of a four-ton locomotive. It was originally named *Hero*, but soon afterwards rechristened *Peppersass* because of its resemblance to a pepper sauce bottle, then a commonly used item on dining tables.

On August 29, 1866, several dozen invited railroad officials, stockholders, and newspaper reporters gathered at the Base Station, where they were pushed up and lowered down a section of test track by this small, but powerful engine. Having proved such a scheme would work, Marsh received valuable financial support from the Boston, Concord, and Montreal Railroad, which also agreed to extend its tracks the 25-mile distance from Littleton to the Cog Railway's starting point.

With Sylvester Marsh as its president, the Mount Washington Steam Railway Company pressed ahead with construction over the next three years, finally reaching the summit on July 3, 1869. When it was completed, the Cog Railway had cost $125,000 to build, and had utilized 700,000 feet of timber and 230 tons of iron in the nearly 3 miles of wooden trestle work needed to support Marsh's specially designed track. The line had an average grade of 25 percent and a maximum grade of 37 percent on the famous section of elevated trestle known as

"Jacob's Ladder," where engine and car were suspended high in the air while being pitched at an incredible angle. As might be expected, the opening of the Cog Railway caused a sensation, with some 60,000 people carried to the mountaintop during its first eight years of operation. This excerpt from an August 21, 1869, article in *Harper's Weekly* gives some idea of the excitement generated by what quickly became one of America's foremost tourist attractions:

> We start. There are no words—only looks, one at another, and underhand graspings of the seat; and up, up we go, as if pushed from the earth into the air. No place to step off upon. On a trestle-work, sometimes more than twenty feet high, we seem entirely severed from the earth. The stoutest of the party looks a little pale; but we feel the firm grip of cog upon cog; we remember that the wheel is so clamped upon the pin-rigged middle rail that neither the engine nor the car can be lifted or thrown off; that the pawl dropped into the rachet-wheel would hold us in the steepest place; that the shutting of a valve in the atmospheric brakes effectually stops the wheels from moving; we look at our Superintendent, who stands composedly watching the engine; his calmness inspires us with courage, and we dare to look off, and then—we forget all fears.

An interesting footnote to Sylvester Marsh's work at Mount Washington has to do with later mountain-climbing railways, most especially those built in

The brainchild of Sylvester Marsh, the Mount Washington Cog Railway was completed in 1869 as the world's first mountain-climbing railroad. It remains a highly popular tourist attraction today.

Switzerland. Offering his advice and patents *gratis* to the Swiss locomotive works manager Niklaus Riggenbach in 1869, Marsh declined an opportunity to become Riggenbach's partner in the development of Europe's first cog railway. He instead allowed his pioneering invention on Mount Washington to serve as a model for the famed Mount Rigi Railway, which opened on May 21, 1871. Although modifications and improvements to Marsh's original designs were carried out in the construction of over 50 cog railways built throughout the world, almost all have followed Swiss designs based on Marsh's original patents dating from the 1860s.

The opening of the Mount Washington Carriage Road in 1861 and Cog Railway in 1869 coincided with the widespread availability of paper photographs in America, a situation that proved highly profitable to the handful of photographers then working in the region. Easily duplicated through the use of collodion negatives and albumen prints, such photographs were less expensive than paintings, yet served equally well as visual reminders of a trip into the mountains. By the time of the Civil War, stereographs, which when viewed with a "stereoscope" produced a three-dimensional image, had become extremely popular as souvenirs, and a growing number of photographers, including the Bierstadt brothers of New Bedford, Massachusetts, and the Kilburn brothers of Littleton, were soon producing thousands of images of the wonders of the White Mountains.

The harmonious integration of nature and machinery held a special fascination for an American public entering the Gilded Age, and tourists eagerly paid for photographs showing Sylvester Marsh's Cog Railway clambering up the steep, boulder-strewn side of Mount Washington. In September 1869, President Ulysses

In 1876 the Boston, Concord, and Montreal Railroad was extended to the Cog Railway Base Station, making it possible to travel by rail from East Coast cities to the top of Mount Washington.

S. Grant took advantage of the Cog Railway's remarkable popularity by having his picture taken several times during a trip up Mount Washington. So prevalent was this new image-making process that by the mid-1870s photographs of White Mountain localities were rapidly replacing woodcuts and engravings in guidebooks and magazine articles. Important marketing tools as well as travel mementos, these early photographs were especially valued for their potential to document reality. Besides Benjamin and Edward Kilburn, whose Littleton photographic studio eventually became the world's largest producer of stereoscopic views, other photographers of note who began working in the White Mountains at this time were Franklin G. Weller, Henry S. Fifield, Nathan W. Pease, and John P. Soule.

During the early 1870s, the center of White Mountain tourism shifted back to the west side of Mount Washington as the Cog Railway drew travelers away from Gorham and the Glen. Amazed by the number of people flocking to the Cog's Base Station, one observer of the tourist trade exclaimed in 1875, "The success which has attended the enterprise has been so marked as to almost revolutionize the travel in the mountain region." Sylvester Marsh had wisely foreseen the need for a large hotel somewhere near the railway's lower terminus, and in 1872–1873, the Mount Washington Hotel Company, with Marsh at its head, erected a three-story, T-shaped building opposite the turnpike entrance leading directly to the Cog. Christened the Fabyan House in honor of Horace Fabyan, who had managed the Mount Washington House here until 1853, the new hotel occupied the site of the Giant's Grave, a glacial prominence that was removed, amid protests, to allow for construction of the 500-guest facility. According to newspaper reports, most of the debate surrounding the obliteration of that famous White Mountain landmark centered around an ancient curse uttered by an Indian standing atop the mound and waving a burning pitch-pine torch kindled at a tree struck by lighting: "No paleface shall take deep root here; this the Great Spirit whispered in my ear." Although two earlier hotels built here had burned in succession, the Fabyan House would seemingly defy the curse by lasting well into the twentieth century, disappearing in a fiery conflagration in 1951.

Making good on its earlier promise, the Boston, Concord, and Montreal Railroad finally reached "Fabyan's" by way of Wing Road and Bethlehem Junction on July 4, 1874; two years later, the railroad was extended 6 miles further to "Marshfield," as the Cog's Base Station was now called. In order for conventional trains to climb the steep grade between Fayban's and the base—amounting to an elevation difference of 1,150 feet—a special, 29-ton Mogul locomotive was constructed by the Manchester Locomotive Works. The opening of this all-important railroad link made it possible for tourists to travel directly by rail from the country's cities to the top of Mount Washington. Once there, Victorian travelers could dine in style and find comfortable overnight accommodations at a new Summit House, a huge two-and-a-half story wooden hotel erected by the Cog Railway in 1872–1873 to replace the woefully inadequate stone shelters of the early 1850s.

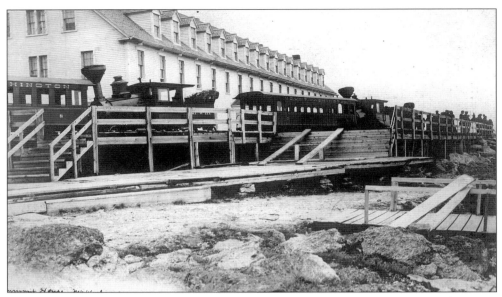

The second Mount Washington Summit House was the largest American hotel on any mountain of such height when it opened in 1873. The hotel was the centerpiece of the summit colony until 1908.

Proclaimed as the largest hotel in the country on any mountain of such height at the time of its opening, the second Summit House boasted a 150-seat dining room, nearly 100 "sleeping rooms," and its own orchestra. Costing some $60,000 to build (a debt that was soon eliminated by capacity crowds), the massive edifice required some 250 freight trains of construction materials, and had its heavy wooden framework securely bolted to the summit rocks, a sensible precaution inasmuch as the building was subjected to winds of up to 186 miles per hour in later years. Among the more notable guests who visited the Summit House during its heyday were President and Mrs. Rutherford B. Hayes, Reverend and Mrs. Henry Ward Beecher, General George McClellan, Admiral Robert E. Peary, and showman Phineas T. Barnum, who supposedly declared the view from the mountaintop "The Second Greatest Show on Earth."

Often compared to the Cog Railway in its engineering difficulty was laying out the Portland and Ogdensburg Railroad through Crawford Notch in the mid-1870s. Organized by a group of Maine businessmen in 1867, this line began in Portland and was designed to be a competitor to the Grand Trunk, but never reached Ogdensburg, New York, even though connections with other railroads leading westward from its terminus in Vermont were ultimately made. Under head civil engineers John F. Anderson and Charles J. Noyes, construction reached North Conway by the summer of 1871. During 1872 and 1873, the railroad inched its way toward the southern entrance of Crawford Notch, where tracks appeared in the front dooryard of Abel Crawford's old

Mount Crawford House at Bemis in June of 1874. From this location, the Portland and Ogdensburg climbed steadily toward the Gate of the Notch along the western wall of the vast bowl, necessitating much blasting of ledge and hauling of fill to create a pathway wide enough to allow the safe passage of trains. Between Bemis and the Crawford House, the latter situated on a level plain just west of the Gate, the grade would be an impressive 116 feet to the mile for 9 consecutive miles.

Added to the hazards of construction was a need to span two mighty gorges with spectacular iron trestles. Rising 80 feet above the ground for a distance of nearly 500 feet, the Frankenstein Trestle was completed near the south end of the notch in June 1875. Finished a short time later and located some 4 miles further west was Willey Brook Bridge, a 140-foot span suspended 90 feet above a rocky chasm giving way to the depths of the notch far below. Using vast amounts of black powder and primitive hoisting derricks, workers created a shelf along the side of Mount Willard and blasted a "Great Cut" through the ledge on the western side of the Gate.

In August 1875, excursion trains began running to Fabyan's, and the achievement of conquering the notch was celebrated amid tremendous public fanfare. Although the Maine Central would assume control of the financially troubled "Mountain Division" a little more than a decade later, the respect for all those involved in this colossal undertaking has not diminished over time.

The arrival of the Portland and Ogdensburg Railroad in the White Mountains and the construction of a narrow gauge railroad from Bethlehem Junction to the Profile House in 1878–1879 placed many of the region's most popular grand hotels within a short drive (or walk) from rail connections. The availability of

The famous "Giant's Grave" was removed to make way for the Fabyan House, built in 1872–1873. The hotel's guests were primarily tourists using the nearby Mount Washington Cog Railway.

The Portland and Ogdensburg Railroad was built through Crawford Notch in the 1870s. From left are Willey Brook Bridge, the railroad section house, Mount Willard, and Dismal Pool.

these new railroads, not surprisingly, gave impetus for the construction of even more hotels, including the Mount Pleasant House at Bretton Woods, the Maplewood Hotel at Bethlehem, the Sunset Hill House at Sugar Hill, Gray's Inn at Jackson, the Deer Park Hotel at North Woodstock, and the Dix House (after 1895 called The Balsams) at Dixville Notch, among many others. Summing up the general effect of railroads on the White Mountains, historian Frederick W. Kilbourne wrote in 1916:

> There is in this country probably no other summer-resort area, and certainly no other mountain district of anything like its extent, that is today provided with such an abundance of railroad facilities, rendering it at once easy of access and convenient for local travel. Indeed, this is so much the case that it may be affirmed that, like some other parts of New England, it is possibly oversupplied with such means of transportation.

Throughout the railroad era, Mount Washington's summit colony remained a prime destination. Beginning in 1877, the summer newspaper *Among the Clouds* was published twice daily from the top of New England, carrying lists of summit arrivals and news from the leading White Mountain resort hotels. This unique paper was founded by Henry M. Burt of Springfield, Massachusetts, and was initially set up in the Tip-Top House, but in 1884 it moved to its own building containing a fully-equipped printing plant with a Hoe cylinder press. In order to beat the city dailies, the paper was often conveyed down the mountain through the use of "slideboards" or "Devil's Shingles," primitive 1-by-3-foot planks originally developed by Cog Railway workers to rapidly descend Mount Washington at the end of the day, sometimes at speeds averaging 60 miles per hour.

Publication of *Among the Clouds* ceased in 1908 when most of the summit buildings were destroyed in a cataclysmic fire, with it reviving from 1910 to 1918 when it was printed at the Cog Railway Base Station. A rival paper, the *White Mountain Echo and Tourist Register*, appeared in 1878, and was published for many years from an office in Bethlehem's Cruft Block.

By the mid-1870s, Mount Washington's manmade attractions were clearly drawing as much attention as the venerable mountain itself. One of the most fascinating summit features at this time was a sturdy, one-and-a-half story building erected in 1874 and operated as a meteorological station by the United States Signal Service year-round through the winter of 1886–1887, and each summer thereafter until 1892.

The origins of this unusual facility are outlined in a fascinating volume entitled *Mount Washington in Winter* (1871). In 1868, the state legislature greatly advanced scientific knowledge of the White Mountains by authorizing a new geological

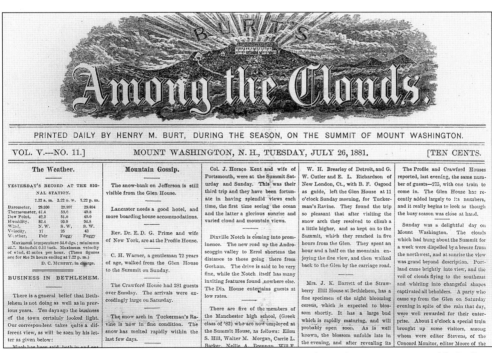

Among the Clouds was the first, and for many years the only, newspaper published on a major American mountaintop. Visitors to Mount Washington's summit were often surprised to find a printing office there.

The U.S. Signal Service erected this heavily braced structure atop Mount Washington in 1874. Weather observations were conducted from this building until 1892.

survey of the state. To carry out the work, Professor Charles H. Hitchcock of Dartmouth College was appointed state geologist, and Joshua H. Huntington of Hanover, and George L. Vose of Paris, Maine, were hired as his assistants. Huntington, especially, had long held a desire to spend a winter atop Mount Washington to make weather observations under what would surely be extremely difficult conditions. When permission was denied to use the Tip-Top House during the winter of 1869–1870 for such an undertaking, Huntington and A.F. Clough, a photographer from Warren, were instead allowed to occupy the Mount Moosilauke Summit House. By all accounts, these daring adventurers were in their element during the two-month stay above the treeline, even when a high wind blew glass out of a window, extinguished the fire, and smashed their hurricane lamp. The following season, Huntington, whose name is attached to a huge glacial cirque on Mount Washington's east side, led a five-man team that endured a grueling winter in the confines of the Cog Railway's summit station, making reports to Hitchcock via a telegraph wire strung down along the railroad trestlework.

This undertaking was so successful the United States Signal Service established a permanent weather observatory in 1871, and much information about the arctic-like conditions in that remote and lonesome place were recorded over the years. Sergeant Winfield Scott Jewell of nearby Lisbon was among the early observers. Stationed atop the mountain from 1878 to 1880, Jewell was a member of the ill-fated Greely Arctic Expedition, being the first to perish from starvation in April 1884. The protection offered by the Signal Service's facility at the summit may have played a part in encouraging the first winter ascent of Mount Washington by women. Describing the three-hour hike up the railway track as "glorious fun," Placentia Crawford Durgin and Eluthera Crawford Freeman, two of Ethan Allen Crawford's daughters, made the trip in February 1874 in the company of their brother, William H. Crawford, and nephew, Ethan Allen Crawford II.

Following on the heels of the State Geological Survey, numerous studies of a scientific and semiscientific nature continued to be carried out in the White Mountains, with valuable articles and books written by such "literary naturalists" as Bradford Torrey, Frank Bolles, Winthrop Packard, William C. Prime, and Annie Trumbull Slosson. Highly knowledgeable about the plants and insects of the higher elevations (she is credited with identifying some 3,000 different insects that at one time inhabited Mount Washington's summit cone), Slosson is best remembered today for her 1898 book *Fishin' Jimmy*, a fictional work set in her beloved Franconia region.

Slosson and her fellow writers helped refocus the public's attention on the unsurpassed natural world of the White Mountains. In addition, their writings also encouraged new attitudes toward the preservation and conservation of forest resources being threatened by widescale timber-cutting operations and related industrialization. As their readers would soon discover, the White Mountains had entered a new era, one filled with perils that made the North Country's severe winter weather look tame by comparison.

Old Jack of the Mountain, White Mountains, N.H.

English Jack was a bewhiskered hermit who spent summers at this shanty near the Gate of the Notch. Crawford House guests purchased his walking staffs and were thrilled with his colorful stories.

7. Times of Transition

The development of lumbering in the White Mountain region is one of the most colorful chapters in the area's past, and can be divided into two distinct periods, with the state's sale in 1867 of some 172,000 acres in the North Country forming a convenient dividing line between them. Previous to this landmark event, which added a mere $25,000 to the state's coffers, logging in the steep-sided valleys of northern New Hampshire and the adjacent parts of western Maine was carried out on a limited scale, with nearly all cutting taking place in the easily accessible lowlands. The prevailing attitude during the era of town settlement was that the forests were an obstruction to agriculture, and therefore should be removed as soon and as rapidly as possible. This sentiment was clearly expressed by Timothy Dwight following his 1797 visit to the White Mountains, when he remarked:

> I am transported in imagination to that period in which, at a little distance, the hills, and plains, and valleys around me will be stripped of the forests which now majestically and even gloomily overshadow them, and be measured out into farms enlivened with all the beauties of cultivation.

Before the Civil War, considerable quantities of white pine destined to become ship masts and spars, as well as sawn lumber, were floated down the Saco, Androscoggin, and Pemigewasset Rivers, which contained a sufficient volume of water for spring drives, despite their many waterfalls. The largest of these log-driving operations was overseen by the famed "New England Timber King," Nicholas G. Norcross, who transported millions of board feet down the Pemigewasset and Merrimack Rivers to a company-owned sawmill in Lowell, Massachusetts, beginning in 1844.

For the most part, however, the majority of waterways in the White Mountains were too shallow and rocky to be utilized in this manner. These twisting rivers and streams instead provided abundant locations for small dams, which held back enough water to power modest-sized sawmills during all but the driest of months. Previous to the coming of the railroads, White Mountain sawmills depended

Large-scale timber operations had a tremendous impact on the White Mountain economy. Brown's Lumber Company at Whitefield was once the largest mill of its kind in New England.

heavily on timberlands that were close at hand, and produced lumber for local consumption only. These limiting circumstances began to change with the arrival of the Atlantic and St. Lawrence Railroad at Gorham in 1851, and accelerated with the completion of other main lines, including the Pemigewasset Valley Railroad between Plymouth and North Woodstock, in 1883, and the Boston and Maine's 20-mile extension between Jefferson Meadows and Berlin, which opened a decade later. Yet it was the sale in the 1860s of substantial tracts of state-owned forest acreage to private interests and land speculators, and the subsequent construction of 17 legally incorporated logging railroads, that made it possible for large-scale timber-cutting operations to gain a powerful grip on the primeval woodlands of the North Country.

In 1870, the narrow-gauge John's River Railroad at Whitefield became the first railway line built specifically to haul logs from the more remote corners of the White Mountains. Converted to standard gauge a few years later, this logging railroad hauled timber to Brown's Lumber Company at Whitefield, which by the mid-1880s ranked as the largest mill of its kind in New England. In 1877, the second logging road in the region appeared when a 2-mile stretch of the Sawyer River Railroad was built west from a connection with the Portland and Ogdensburg Railroad at the southern end of Crawford Notch. Although the Sawyer River Railroad ultimately reached a length of only 9 miles, the line remained active under the Saunders family of Lawrence, Massachusetts, until 1928 to earn the distinction of being the next to last logging railroad to operate in the White Mountains.

Many White Mountain farmers worked in logging camps during the winter. Although logging railroads appeared in 1870, horses and oxen were needed to haul timber down from steep mountainsides.

A combination of easy access, a seemingly inexhaustible supply of timber, and the likelihood for tremendous financial gain were major forces driving the White Mountain logging industry during the 1870s. Additional pressure to cut down the vast stands of spruce and fir then cloaking whole mountainsides came during the following decade, when the sulfite process of reducing softwoods to pulp was introduced in the production of paper.

By the summer of 1885, when the second Glen House opened on the site of its fire-ravaged predecessor, the denuding of the White Hills was well underway, causing hotel guests to voice their objections in the pages of local newspapers and the twice-daily editions of *Among the Clouds*. However, the quantity of virgin timber in the region was so extensive that these complaints went largely unheeded until the late 1880s, when destructive forest fires fed by huge piles of slash and debris ignited the earliest efforts to preserve the forests. In a strange irony, the devouring demands of the lumberman were causing "a condition of extreme desolation" just as unprecedented numbers of people were coming to the mountains to enjoy the district's forested beauty.

If the sudden appearance of logging camps, mill villages, and logging railroads caught the attention of White Mountain tourists and hoteliers of the 1870s and 1880s, the changing landscape was also of concern to a vigorous new generation of recreational walkers and climbers who now poured into the highlands to trek up all of the major peaks. These late Victorian mountain lovers fervently believed in walking as the best way of experiencing the great outdoors. Ministers, teachers, businessmen, and college students (many of the latter from Dartmouth) now made annual pilgrimages to the hills, taking on entire ranges and frequently choosing as their base of operations smaller inns or boarding houses that were more affordable and, like the much beloved Ravine House in Randolph, removed from the grandiosity of hotel life. These mostly middle-class adventurers, among whom were many women, initiated a sustained period of trail construction in the White Mountains that was the first of its kind in America.

Although a cluster of hiking paths to several mountain peaks encircling Waterville Valley was built by local innkeeper Nathaniel Greeley before the Civil War, the first modern hiking trail in the White Mountains did not appear until 1875–1876. Charles E. Lowe of Randolph, at the behest of summer resident William G. Nowell, opened a route up the north side of Mount Adams that became the first fully cleared trail on the Northern Presidentials. A flurry of footpath construction, much of it under the auspices of the newly formed Appalachian Mountain Club, followed this pioneering effort and lasted well into the second decade of the twentieth century. Many of the principal trails created during this time were located in the Moat Range, above the Albany Intervale, up the East Branch of the Pemigewasset River, in Crawford and Franconia Notches, and near Randolph.

In the 1870s, the Ravine House in Randolph, New Hampshire, became headquarters for an enthusiastic group of hikers building trails onto the northern Presidentials. The hotel was demolished in 1962.

121

It was also in the 1870s that the first organized hiking clubs devoted to climbing in the White Mountains were formed. Predating the Appalachian Mountain Club by three years, the White Mountain Club of Portland came together in 1873 under the energetic personalities of John F. Anderson, chief engineer of the Portland and Ogdensburg Railroad; Abner Lowell, one of the early instigators of the Mount Washington Carriage Road; George L. Vose, assistant to Charles Hitchcock in the recent geological survey of New Hampshire; and Harrison Bird Brown, an artist known well for his superb White Mountain scenes. The second mountaineering organization of its type in North America (earlier was the 1863 short-lived Alpine Club of Williamstown, Massachusetts) and the first of any consequence in the White Mountains, the White Mountain Club of Portland organized many expeditions into hitherto unexplored parts of northern New Hampshire and western Maine. The wild and rugged Mahoosuc Range, extending from Gorham east to Grafton Notch, was a favorite locale of the group.

During the mid-1870s, members of the White Mountain Club also made a number of trips to Mount Carrigain, often under the leadership of the indefatigable Major John Mead Gould, author of the classic 1877 hiking manual, *How to Camp Out*. The names of some of the most prominent early members of this hiking organization are recalled today in three of the main peaks overlooking the Carrigain Notch wilderness: Mount Lowell, Mount Anderson, and Vose Spur. Despite its auspicious beginnings, the ebullience of the White Mountain Club of Portland seems to have dwindled after 1880 when the more broadly based Appalachian Mountain Club (AMC) had come to dominate "the exploration, study, and pleasure use of the White Mountains."

On January 8, 1876, at a meeting held on the campus of the Massachusetts Institute of Technology in Boston, the AMC was formed. Officially incorporated on March 13, 1878, the AMC is now the oldest continuously operating mountain-climbing organization in the United States. Created "for the advancement of the interests of those who visit the mountains of New England and adjacent regions, whether for the purpose of scientific research or summer recreation," the AMC was steered during its early years by a coterie of highly talented and unusually ambitious mountain enthusiasts, including Samuel H. Scudder, Charles E. Fay, William G. Nowell, J. Rayner Edmands, and brothers Edward C. and William H. Pickering. Professor Edward Pickering, then a teacher of physics at MIT, is credited with developing the idea for the club and served as its first president. His successor, Samuel Scudder, suggested the idea of a regular club publication. Titled *Appalachia*, it is now America's longest running journal of mountaineering and conservation.

Much of the prestige connected with the AMC's first days came largely from the work of two of its leaders, Charles H. Hitchcock and Joshua H. Huntington, who received accolades for their knowledge of White Mountain topography well before the club's existence. Perhaps the most visible sign of the AMC's work in the White Mountains during a long period of backcountry stewardship

The second mountaineering organization in North America was the White Mountain Club of Portland. Two winter hikers make their way up Mount Washington's summit cone about 1915.

has been the construction of a series of overnight shelters patterned after those found in Europe and spaced a day's hike apart. The earliest of these, Madison Spring Hut, was erected in 1888 of native stone in the col (valley) between Mounts Madison and Adams. This trail-side system, which stretches from Franconia Notch in the west to Carter Notch in the east, has evolved to include eight mountain hostels.

Other AMC facilities operating today in the White Mountains include the Cold River Camp, a former church retreat center on Route 113 south of Evans Notch, which was donated to the club in 1919 by Theodore Conant of Boston; the club's Pinkham Notch Visitor Center, opened in 1920 and greatly enlarged since; and the Crawford Hostel and Visitor Center, which offers easy access to endless backcountry from the site of the old Crawford House hotel.

Looking back at the formative years of the Appalachian Mountain Club, it seems clear the activities of this association influenced the creation of many smaller, though no less robust, hiking organizations in the White Mountains before World War II. The clubs that particularly stood out were the Wonalancet Out Door Club, Chocorua Mountain Club, Waterville Athletic and Improvement Association, Randolph Mountain Club, and the North Woodstock Improvement Association.

The growth of mountain recreation during the 1870s spawned the publication of a new type of guidebook, one where the main focus was on climbing routes

In the 1890s, the Wild River Lumber Company built a logging railroad from Gilead, Maine, into the forested valleys east of the Carter-Moriah Range. The railroad ceased operations in 1904.

rather than general travel itineraries by road or railroad. The first of these guides was published in 1876, the same year the Appalachian Mountain Club was organized, and was titled *The White Mountains: A Handbook for Travellers* (but labeled *Osgood's White Mountains* on the cover). The book was penned by Moses Foster Sweetser of Boston, who later wrote the text for *Views in the White Mountains* (1879), *Chisholm's White Mountain Guide-Book* (1880), and *The White Mountain Region of New England* (1888), the latter published by the Boston and Maine Railroad. Sweetser claimed to have ascended more than 80 White Mountain peaks to prepare his 1876 *Handbook*, which appeared in many editions and was not displaced until the Appalachian Mountain Club began issuing its own guide to the region's trails in 1907. Sweetser's extremely detailed *Handbook* not only suggested how and where to hike, but why one should take to the hills in the first place:

> When the busy citizen has grown weary under the pressure of business or study, and loses his ability to eat or sleep, or to take pleasure either in present or anticipated comforts, let him visit the mountains and inhale their electric air, forgetting for the month his home-cares, and adapting his thoughts to the ennobling surroundings. The sojourn in a summer-hotel is well and beneficial, but the journey

on foot is better, since it gives incessant variety and ever-changing themes of diversion. After a few days of marching, he will cease to complain of sleepless nights or zestless meals, and will find the leathery steaks of the village-inns more delicious than the choicest triumphs of the Parisian *chefs*. The pedestrian tour is of high value to men of sedentary habits, giving them a valuable and needed change of habit, expanding their shrunken lungs, and teaching their limbs pliancy and strength. It is pleasing to see so many of the undergraduates of the New England colleges taking up this form of exercise and visiting the mountains in small squads on active service. In the course of time it may be that the White Mountains shall be as favorite [a] walking-ground as the Scottish Highlands or Swiss Alps now are, and that the nervous American energy may acquire a legitimate strengthening of solid Anglo-Saxon endurance.

The years between establishing the New Hampshire Forestry Commission in 1883 and passing the Weeks Act of 1911, authorizing federal purchases of forest lands to protect valuable watersheds, were characterized by a growing awareness of the need to safeguard the significant natural resources of the White Mountains. Farming had given way to logging as the region's economic mainstay by 1886, when paper was produced for the first time in Berlin, a flourishing center of manufacturing on the Androscoggin. Tourism continued to grow throughout the period, with over 200 summer inns and hotels in operation by 1890. Not

Burgess Sulphite Paper Mill, Berlin, N. H.

At one time, the pulp and paper industry in Berlin, New Hampshire, employed more people than any other enterprise in Coos County. Paper was produced here for the first time in 1886.

unexpectedly, clashes between those who wished to save the forests and those who wanted to cut them down intensified as logging activity reached a fevered pitch just before the turn of the century.

Of the many hard driving lumber barons who created empires in the White Mountains during this turbulent era, perhaps none was more maligned in his day than James Everell (J.E.) Henry, known variously as the "Wood Butcher" and the "Grand Duke of Lincoln." Beginning in the mid-1870s, Henry and his partners acquired extensive timberlands in the Zealand River Valley lying south of present-day Route 302 between Twin Mountain and Bretton Woods. Here, in a wilderness tract untouched by man, the greatest of the White Mountain lumber kings first demonstrated his shrewd business skill and ceaseless appetite for trees.

By 1884, a standard-gauge logging railroad had been constructed alongside the Zealand River, and the mill village of "Zealand," complete with sawmill, workers' houses, post office, boarding house, and company store had sprung up on the banks of the Ammonoosuc River where the Zealand Valley Railroad connected with the tracks of the Boston, Concord, and Montreal Railroad. At least six logging camps, whose crews included many Irish, Swedes, Italians, Poles, and French-Canadians, among other nationalities, were constructed along dug-way roads fanning out into the more isolated corners of the Zealand Valley not accessible by the railroad. The workmen and their horses spent 11-hour days in the woods hauling out spruce timber, the most desired species of the time. The

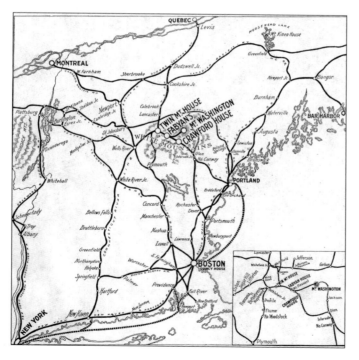

By the close of the nineteenth century, the White Mountain tourist industry had attained remarkable economic success due to the convenience of railroads. This map of rail routes appeared in a Crawford House brochure.

work was tough, the pay decent (about $6 a week and board), and the camp food plentiful.

Logging activity in the Zealand Valley continued unabated until the summer of 1886, when sparks from one of J.E. Henry's Baldwin engines ignited a forest fire that, in a week's time, destroyed some 12,000 acres, much of it involving timber yet to be harvested. Since the area burned was dangerously close to several of the region's resort hotels, the public clamor to halt frenzied destruction of the forests now became louder, but little could be done as Henry and other timber moguls were cutting on private property.

By 1892, Henry had exhausted what remained of the timber supply in the Zealand Valley and transferred his equipment and crews south to the thickly forested wilderness encompassing the East Branch of the Pemigewasset River, where he virtually founded the town of Lincoln and its once thriving timber-cutting and paper-making operations. The efficiency of Henry's clear-cutting operations in this section of the White Mountains resulted in whole mountainsides being stripped bare, the scars of "upper roads" visible from many miles away. Such heavy logging, which caused severe erosion and clogged mountain streams with silt, was blamed for spring floods on the Merrimack River in 1895 and 1896 that shut down the Amoskeag Mill in Manchester, leaving 6,000 employees out of work. The temporary closing of the world's largest textile complex caught the public's attention and brought a stinging indictment from the Amoskeag Manufacturing Company's treasurer, T. Jefferson Coolidge, but nothing could change the fact that the North Country's economy now depended on lumbering. The pulp and paper industry in Berlin, "the city that trees built," employed more people than any other enterprise in Coos County.

The power of the pen as a tool for saving the forests, and therefore the very character of the White Mountains, was amply demonstrated in July 1900 when a short pamphlet written by the Reverend John E. Johnson, an Episcopal missionary then stationed in North Woodstock, was published. Entitled *The Boa Constrictor of the White Mountains, or the Worst "Trust" in the World*, Johnson's booklet carried an essay that went beyond the more obvious consequences of deforestation—the spring floods, the thousands of acres burned, and the loss of revenue to the tourist industry—to focus on the privations of those who had been squeezed off the land. Johnson pulled no punches when pointing the finger of blame, as this excerpt from his pamphlet demonstrates:

> What is it? The New Hampshire Land Company. Where is it? Up among the granite hills of that state. What is its object? To deforest and depopulate the region lying around the head waters of the Merrimack River in the heart of the White Mountains. Its history and *modus operandi*? In the early days of the company it was allowed to acquire for a song all the public lands thereabouts, and later to "take over" all tax-titles, until finally there was no considerable tracts in that vicinity which it did not own. . . .

127

The next step was also a process of "refrigeration," and is still going on. It consisted of getting rid of the native population, a hardy stock, who had clung to the home wood lots belonging to the rough areas which they called their farms—for they were more lumbermen than agriculturalists. These must need be driven out to make way for deforesting operations on a large scale. . . .

Summer visitors to this section of the White Mountains have noticed the many deserted farms and dilapidated buildings and have wondered at such scenes, not dreaming that the cause was to be found in the operations of a company *chartered to do it*; that this desolation was due to the gradual tightening of the coils of a boa constrictor *legalized* to crush the human life out of these regions, preparatory to stripping them of their forests; for depopulation here is not due to the causes which have led to the abandonment of farms elsewhere in the state. The inhabitants of this section never depended exclusively upon the scant returns from their rough farms for a living but rather upon their winter's work in the woods, a dependence that never would have been exhausted had they been left in possession, since their methods were those which are now advocated by scientific forestry. The farmer felled some of the largest trees in the woods every winter and hauling them out endwise injured nothing, but rather left the rest better for it. His successor, the professional lumberman, cuts everything, rolls it down the mountain, crushing the saplings, and not content with that, often burns the refuse for charcoal.

Reverend Johnson's well chosen words, written in the muckraking tradition of such "Progressive Era" reformers as Ida Tarbell and Lincoln Steffens, enflamed the public and served as a wake-up call to those who regarded the White Mountains as a national treasure. Among the most prominent of these individuals was New Hampshire Governor Frank W. Rollins, who on February 6, 1901, organized a meeting in Concord to form a citizens' advocacy group specifically aimed at preserving the scenic beauty of the White Mountains. One of the first conservation groups of its type in the country, the Society for the Protection of New Hampshire Forests (SPNHF) hired the energetic Philip W. Ayres as its executive forester in 1902. When fires burned over some 85,000 acres the following spring—one tenth of the total White Mountain area—creating a desolate waste that many living outside the region considered a national dilemma, Ayres led the effort for an end to "unwise and barbarous" lumbering practices and the establishment of a program of sustainable forest management techniques within a government-owned forest reservation. Boosted by a "back-to-nature" movement sweeping through the country at the time and encouraged by President Theodore Roosevelt's efforts to preserve federal lands in the American West, the SPNHF, the New Hampshire Forestry Commission, the Appalachian Mountain Club, and various key political leaders

White Mts. N.H.,
The Tally-Ho leaving the Glen House for Glen Station.

After the second Glen House burned in 1893, the former servants' quarters were fitted up for use by tourists. The barns sheltered horses and mountain wagons used on the Mount Washington Carriage Road.

worked closely together to make the idea of a "White Mountain National Forest" a reality.

Years of debate in Congress ensued, but in 1911, the Appalachian-White Mountains Forest Reservation Bill finally passed. More familiarly known as the "Weeks Act" in honor of John Wingate Weeks, the Massachusetts Congressman and Lancaster native who worked so tirelessly for its enactment, this law authorized the federal government to appropriate funds for the acquisition of lands and forest reserves for "the conservation and improvement of the navigability of a river." Soon after it went into effect, some 30,000 acres, mostly on the northern slopes of the Presidential Range, were purchased as the first segment of a proposed 698,000-acre White Mountain National Forest.

In association with the state, which moved quickly under the threat of timber cutting to purchase and preserve the upper section of Crawford Notch (now part of "Crawford Notch State Park") in 1912, the National Forest Reservation Commission continued to acquire significant parcels, including most of Mount Washington and many other major peaks in the district. The "people's proposition" had succeeded, signaling the ending of one era of White Mountain history and the start of yet another.

The early twentieth century effort that led to safeguarding the forested hills of northern New Hampshire and westernmost Maine strengthened a long-standing belief that the scenic value of the White Mountains should dominate over the region's capacity to supply timber products. However, recognition of the "peculiar character" of these fabled highlands did not signify that lumber interests were to be completely subordinated to scenery. Since establishing a national forest, as opposed to a national park, allowed harvesting timber under the principle of continuous yield while developing recreation, propagating wildlife, protecting watersheds, and preserving the area's special areas (activities now grouped under the designation of "multiple use management"), lumber mills and wood-working factories were secure. In fact, the last of the logging railroads in the White Mountains, the East Branch and Lincoln Railroad, continued to haul small loads of spruce and fir out of the "Pemigewasset Wilderness" backcountry until the summer of 1947.

Widespread timber-cutting operations at the turn of the century may have outraged fashionable vacationers, but such alterations to the landscape did not preclude the White Mountains from achieving even greater prominence during this time as one of the nation's top resort destinations. In a rural playground largely created by and for urbanites, many of whom now sent their children to exclusive summer camps in the region, the various grand hotels continued to entertain their guests on a lavish scale. During the 1890s, when it was estimated that some 12,000 people could be housed overnight in the region, such improvements as electric lights, telephones, and private baths were introduced at many of the area's largest hotel complexes.

By 1895, the recreational opportunities offered to well-heeled Victorians included tandem bicycling and the game of golf, the national pastime of Scotland. Among the earliest golf courses laid out in the White Mountains and still in use today were those at the Waumbek Hotel in Jefferson, at Wentworth Hall in Jackson, at the Mount Pleasant House in Bretton Woods, and at the Maplewood Hotel in Bethlehem. By the late 1890s, baseball was also a much favored part of grand hotel life, although here the teams were usually made up of college students working at the resorts, rather than hotel guests. Around 1887, "coaching parades" were introduced as the ultimate highlight of the summer social season. These brilliant pageants featured processions of elaborately decorated horse-drawn stages sponsored by the grand hotels that drew thousands of spectators annually to the "East Side" community of North Conway and "West Side" resort town of Bethlehem. A number of coaching parades were also held in Lancaster and Littleton, and special trains were supplied to accommodate crowds of day visitors who journeyed to the mountains for these gala events.

By 1900, the White Mountain hotel industry had attained an unprecedented level of economic success, and in many ways was setting the standard for similar enterprises across the country. Catering to the rich and famous had become commonplace in the North Country, and many of the area's older establishments, like the Mountain View House in Whitefield and The Balsams at Dixville Notch, were greatly expanded and updated to meet the needs of a discriminating clientele. In an extreme example of keeping up with the times, one of the region's largest and oldest hotels, the Profile House at Franconia Notch, was completely demolished in October 1905 so a more modern facility could be opened on the same site the following July. Yet Bretton Woods, renowned for its broad valley and spectacular panorama of the Presidential Range, achieved the pinnacle of White Mountain hotel-keeping in 1902, a century after Eleazer Rosebrook's nearby tavern opened as the first hostelry in the heart of the mountains.

During the 1880s, the wealthy New York-based capitalist Joseph Stickney had become owner of the Mount Pleasant House, a sprawling hotel complex begun in 1875 on the west side of the Ammonoosuc River at Bretton Woods. At the suggestion of John Anderson, then co-proprietor of the Mount Pleasant and son of the man responsible for opening the railroad through Crawford Notch, Stickney and his business partners embarked on an ambitious project to construct a massive hotel atop a prominent ridge in the center of the Ammonoosuc Valley. During the summer of 1901, the site for the "Mount Washington Hotel" was prepared, and construction of the massive granite foundation and framework was pushed forward under the efforts of 250 Italian laborers specially hired for their

Grand hotel guests became enamored with golf during the 1890s. The course at Jefferson's Waumbek Hotel, shown here, was laid out in 1895 and is one of the oldest in the mountains.

skills in carpentry, masonry, and stained glass. On July 28, 1902, the fiftieth anniversary of the opening of Mount Washington's first Summit House, the doors of this palatial hotel, today the *grande dame* of White Mountain resorts, were opened to the public.

Designed in the Spanish Renaissance Revival style by the New York architect Charles Alling Gifford, the Mount Washington Hotel was then, and is now, the largest wooden structure ever erected in New Hampshire. With its five-story octagonal towers, 900-foot veranda, exquisite interior appointments, and 600-guest capacity, it won tremendous acclaim from newspapers and travel magazines for providing the ultimate in gracious hospitality. By building this magnificent hotel, Joseph Stickney, who died unexpectedly in 1903, also created a monument to one of the most significant eras of the region's past. In recognition of Stickney's great achievement and the survival of this imposing structure to the present, the National Park Service has designated the Mount Washington Hotel a "National Historic Landmark."

Under the widowed Carolyn Foster Stickney (who married French nobleman Prince Clarigny de Lucinge in 1908), the Mount Washington Hotel remained one of the Northeast's leading summer resorts into the 1930s when its management passed to others. A major reason for this uninterrupted success was that Joseph Stickney had wisely anticipated the coming of the automobile as an alternative to rail transportation, for not only did the Mount Washington boast a special entrance for automobiles, but also attendant facilities for the storage and maintenance of these newfangled "motor-cars."

Although automobiles first began to appear in the North Country during the 1890s, it was not until one of these horseless carriages ascended to the top of

Before World War I, "auto parades" were all the rage. The originator of the Mount Washington Hotel anticipated the popularity of the automobile by planning for special storage and maintenance facilities.

New England on August 31, 1899, that newspapers and magazines covering the comings and goings in this popular resort area made much of their presence. On that late summer's day, as noted in *Among the Clouds*, Mr. and Mrs. Freelan O. Stanley of Newton, Massachusetts, climbed to the summit of Mount Washington in their steam-powered "Locomobile" in the unheard of time of two hours and ten minutes. News of this astounding feat was immediately sent out to the national press and cabled across the Atlantic so it could appear in the evening's Paris edition of the *New York Herald*. Frank H. Burt, who had just become the editor of *Among the Clouds* upon the death of his father Henry, rather cautiously predicted:

> A new epoch of mountain travel begins from the present day. . . . Compared with the great mass of tourists, those who will come by auto will be necessarily limited in number, but they will form an ever increasing factor in White Mountain travel.

Few people, including Burt, could have foreseen in 1899 how swiftly Americans would take to this new mode of transportation, or to what degree travel and tourism in the White Mountains would change over the next few decades because of it. When, in 1904, the first of a series of National Hill Climbing Competitions was held on the Mount Washington Carriage Road (the name was officially changed to "Auto Road" in 1911), automobiles were still viewed by many Americans as a curiosity. But the flexibility and independence afforded by the automobile made it ideal for vacationers who wished to explore on their own, rather than spend their entire holiday at one hotel or be tied to railroad timetables.

The advent of auto touring, like the coming of the railroads 50 years earlier, transformed the region in dramatic ways to the dismay of many who viewed such fast-paced rambles as an intrusion into the exclusive world of the grand hotels. Yet the excitement and satisfaction generated by the automobile was difficult to escape, as evidenced by writer Ralph D. Paine's comments in a 1913 issue of *Scribner's Magazine*:

> In other days many of the finest views of this beautiful region were denied the visitor unless he tramped it with a pack on his back. Now the hillsides have been blasted and the gullies filled to make it no more than a flight of a few hours from the Franconia gateway, across the mountains and out through Crawford Notch to the highway that leads southward through North Conway and Intervale. Gone is the old simplicity and quiet summer life of Fabyan's and Bethlehem and Crawford's, when the same guests returned year after year for the same placid existence, the young people at tennis and walking tours, their elders gossiping in rocking-chairs along the hospitable piazzas. Nor is it to regret the passing of the old order of things. Where one pilgrim discovered the

The Russell Cottages still exist in Kearsarge village near North Conway. Hundreds of small hotels and boarding houses once dotted the White Mountains.

White Mountains then, a hundred enjoy them now. The region has ceased to be a New England monopoly and is a national possession. At Bretton Woods and its vast hotel, seventy per cent of last summer's guests were motorists.

The "passing of the old order" may have been symbolized by a growing acceptance of the automobile as the preferred way of "doing" the White Mountains, but for many people with long ties to the area it was a catastrophe in 1908 that truly signified the end of an epoch. Early in the evening of June 18, just as many families were sitting down for supper, telephones throughout the region began to ring, spreading the news that the summit colony atop Mount Washington was on fire. So beloved had this mountaintop community become to the residents in surrounding towns, and to New Englanders in general, that few could believe reports coming from the Glen House and Fabyan's, where the flames were first thought to be a reflection of the setting sun on the summit hotel's windows. Unfortunately, this was not the case.

From unknown causes, a fire had broken out in the Summit House, which was being prepared for opening earlier in the day, but was locked tight when a party of hikers staying the night in the Stage Office discovered smoke pouring from some upper story windows. With a stiff wind blowing against the building from the west, there was nothing that could be done to halt the blaze, and soon the entire building was a raging inferno. So quickly did the fire spread, that within a few hours every structure, except for the Tip-Top House and the two Carriage Road

Company stables located just below the summit, had been reduced to a smoldering pile of ashes.

Among the buildings lost were the Summit House, the Stage Office, the unused Signal Service Station, the Cog Railway engine house and car barn, and the newspaper office of *Among the Clouds*. Although the Tip-Top House was immediately pressed into service after the Great Fire of 1908, bringing a nostalgic pleasure to former visitors "that they never dreamed of realizing," the conflagration had destroyed something more than just a widely known cluster of buildings atop Mount Washington. With the disappearance of the Summit House and most of its neighboring structures, a way of life in the White Mountains more closely connected to the primitive past than to the onrushing age of the automobile had vanished forever.

On June 18, 1908, an era of summer hospitality on Mount Washington came to an end when every building in the summit colony, save for the Tip-Top House and two barns, was destroyed by fire.

8. The Enduring Highlands

In the years preceding World War I, major changes in American lifestyles had a striking effect on travel and tourism in the White Mountains. The demand for railroad passenger service, so necessary to the survival of the grand hotels, declined at a steady rate as more and more people came to enjoy the freedom of the road in their own vehicles. These "motorists," many of whom had moderate incomes, now wandered through mountain towns and villages at leisure, sometimes staying for one or two nights at campgrounds or in roadside cottages before journeying off to inspect other parts of the rural Northeast. Because tourists were now liberated from the constraints of travel by rail, they began to think of the tour itself as the vacation, and lengthy stays in grand hotels were increasingly viewed as old fashioned and out of step with the twentieth century.

Recognizing the economic benefits to be gained from this influx of middle-income travelers into the White Mountain region, the states of Maine and New Hampshire, as well as the federal government, encouraged auto tourism in the scenic highlands by spending generous amounts of money on better highways and auto-related tourist services. In 1915, the former homestead of Hayes and Dolly Copp and other nearby farms at the northern entrance to Pinkham Notch were added to the White Mountain National Forest preserve. By 1921, an auto campground—now one of the largest and most popular in the entire National Forest system—had been formally laid out at this picturesque location in the Peabody River Valley.

The arrival of swelling numbers of auto enthusiasts contributed to the demise of the traditional White Mountain vacation, but other influences also fostered this decline. The rising popularity of private cottages, the high cost of maintaining aging wooden hotels, the enactment of the federal income tax, and the onset of a general business recession in New England were some of the factors working against prolonging the conventional mountain holiday. In particular, the growing economic uncertainty of the pre-War period, in conjunction with fears of over-commercialization in the region, was directly responsible for abandoning immediate plans for a massive three-story steel and concrete hotel atop Mount Washington to replace the second Summit House destroyed in 1908.

Mount Washington's third Summit House stood atop "The Rockpile" from 1915 till 1980. The stone Tip-Top House, which survived the Great Fire of 1908, displays its gabled roof, now removed.

This ambitious proposal, based on studies carried out by the Concord and Montreal Railroad between 1910 and 1913, had an estimated cost of well over $1 million and featured a 20-mile electric scenic railway that, if built, would have replaced the Cog and carried passengers over Mounts Jefferson and Clay as it approached the great summit cone from the north. When the third Summit House was ultimately constructed from 1914 to 1915, it was designed on a more modest scale and with day visitors, rather than overnight guests, in mind. Officially dedicated on August 22, 1915, amid the cheers of a large crowd of dignitaries and spectators, the heavily timbered story-and-a-half edifice contained a lobby and dining room on the first floor and a number of small bedrooms in the second, attic story. Like its larger predecessor, the new hotel was fastened down to the summit ledge with iron bolts, allowing it to safely withstand 65 years of sub-arctic gales atop "The Rockpile" until replaced in 1980 by the steel and concrete Sherman Adams Summit Building.

The effects of America's entry into World War I were felt in the White Mountains as elsewhere in the nation. Because many regular employees at the region's resorts and attractions were now involved in the war effort, a number of local hotels shortened their season, and the Cog Railway was shut down completely in 1918. However, by 1920, when the Appalachian Mountain Club opened a North Country base of operations at the eastern foot of Mount Washington, White Mountain tourism had returned to a more normal pace.

North Conway's White Mountain Camps catered to a new breed of tourist interested in "auto touring." Several auto campgrounds, such as Dolly Copp, were also established on National Forest lands.

In order to provide gas, food, and lodging to "automobile parties," shrewd entrepreneurs set up filling stations, restaurants, lunch stands, tea houses, motor courts, cabin villages, and campgrounds alongside all of the region's major highways. In 1922, the state leased the site of the Willey House, destroyed by fire in September 1899, to two Bartlett men who erected a number of small buildings made from peeled spruce logs. "Donahue and Hamlin's Willey House Camps" included a restaurant, gift shop, and several overnight cabins, some of which survive today. Further west, at the southern entrance to Franconia Notch, the Indian Head Resort with its now-famous observation tower came into being at about this same time. The focus of this "auto park" was the prominent stone profile atop nearby 2,554-foot Mount Pemigewasset; it was founded by Ray Gordon, a colorful and energetic showman who eventually erected 74 "English-style cottages" for the comfort of his guests. In a booklet entitled *Indian Head: Its Debut and Legends* (1923), the Reverend Guy Roberts of Whitefield described the wide range of diversions available at this "ideal vacation spot" soon after its opening:

> The tourist's attention is duly called to this great natural curiosity by a steel observation tower 72 feet high, located by the roadside at the spot where the best view of the [Indian] Head is to be obtained.
>
> Near by is a large and well equipped souvenir store and lunchroom, also a much needed filling station for the accommodation of motorists

ere they make the seven hundred foot climb to the height of the Notch near Echo Lake, six and nine tenths miles distant.

Chained near the observation tower are several native black bears which are sure to attract the tourist's notice and likely bits of food, for altho captured from the wild in the woods in the summer of 1921, they have taken to civilization kindly and are safe to approach to within feeding distance. At the tower or the souvenir store can be purchased bottles of "Bear Special," a harmless drink that the bears greatly enjoy while greatly amusing the tourist who may wish to thus treat his bruin friends. These bears can hardly be called "teetotalers" for three of them have a record of having together drunk over 250 bottles of "Special" in one day! Lucky for them that the 18th amendment has been adopted!

In 1930, one of the black bears at Indian Head was purchased by Edward P. Clark, who, with his wife Florence, had opened "Ed Clark's Eskimo Dog Ranch" two years earlier at a spot a few miles further south. Originally established for the purpose of raising and exhibiting Eskimo sled dogs (on April 3, 1932, Mrs. Clark became the first woman to ascend Mount Washington by dog sled without assistance), Clark's

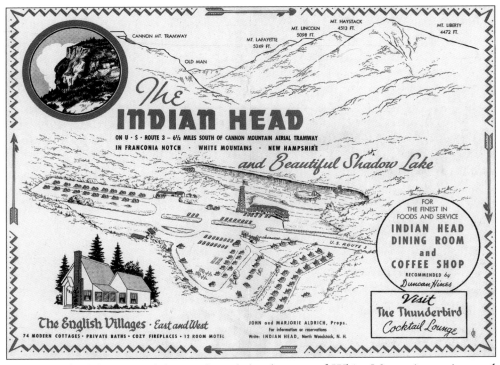

The coming of the automobile transformed the character of White Mountain tourism and caused the demise of the grand hotels. The cottage colony at Indian Head is one of the oldest in the region.

added three more bear cubs in 1935, and in 1949 brothers and sons Edward M. and W. Murray began to train the bears to perform for the public. Today, as "Clark's Trading Post," this forerunner of the many amusement centers and fun parks located in the White Mountains carries on a proud tradition of "Gold Standard Entertainment" with the help of the third and fourth generations of the Clark family. In addition to taking in the bear show, modern day visitors to this engaging roadside attraction can view an impressive collection of antique fire engines, wagons, and coin-operated nickelodeons. Recalling the days of local timber baron J.E. Henry, guests can also enjoy a 30-minute excursion behind a 1921 Climax locomotive formerly used on the nearby East Branch and Lincoln Railroad.

Besides his Indian Head booklet, Reverend Guy Roberts compiled a number of other short works concerning popular White Mountain topics as part of his "Natural Curiosity Series." Among these were *The Flume and All About It* (1923), *The Profile and How It Was Saved* (1924), *"The Great Carbuncle," "Christus Judex,"* and *"The Great Stone Face"* (1924), *The Willey Slide: Its History, Legend, and Romance* (1925), *Mt. Washington: Its Past and Present* (1927), *Old Peppersass: Her Invention and Life Story* (1930), and *Lost River and Going Thru It* (1938). Illustrated with numerous old photos, these moderately-priced, pocket-sized pamphlets were especially aimed at the auto tourist market, in the same way that more extensive guidebooks decorated with woodcuts and engravings were created a half century earlier for hotel quests spending an entire season in the mountains. Through his

Destruction of the second Profile House in 1923 set in motion a series of events that culminated with the creation of Franconia Notch State Park in 1928.

research and writing, Reverend Roberts may have acquainted a new generation with many of the time-honored stories and legends about the White Hills, but it is for his role in the first repairs to the Old Man of the Mountain, the "American Wonder of the World," that he is best remembered today.

In 1906, Reverend Roberts bravely climbed to the top of the Old Man of the Mountain and determined that the forehead boulder was at risk of falling and striking the ledge forming the Old Man's nose. Roberts was well aware of the Profile's importance to New Hampshire and the White Mountain region in general, and over the next decade he actively petitioned the state as well as the owners of the Profile House (who then held title to Cannon Mountain) to take the steps necessary to save the Old Man from the elements. After years of being told that nothing could be done, in 1915 Roberts brought this problem to the attention of Edward H. Geddes, a Quincy, Massachusetts, granite quarry superintendent then visiting relatives in Littleton. Geddes made a trip to the top of the Old Man with Roberts and, based on his examination of the 25-ton forehead stone, soon thereafter designed three heavy turnbuckles that would serve as hinges, allowing the slipping rock to move upward on the ice during the winter, but returning it to its original position when the ice thawed out. Installed the following year, these turnbuckles have been supplemented with a newer system of tie rods, cables, and epoxy-coated wire membranes in a continuing effort to forestall the inexorable forces of ice and gravity. In 1965, responsibility for preserving the Old Man was assigned to the late Niels Nielsen, whose son David, involved since 1969 in this much-publicized effort, is now official caretaker of the Great Stone Face. (The Old Man collapsed while this book was in press.)

Only a few years after efforts to preserve the Old Man of the Mountain began, an even greater threat to his Franconia Notch domain suddenly appeared when the Profile House complex, including all of its guest cottages, burned to the ground. Opened in 1906 at the base of Cannon Mountain, this elegant hostelry was one of the most popular summer resorts in the White Mountains when it was mysteriously destroyed by fire on August 2, 1923, the same day President Warren G. Harding died unexpectedly in San Francisco. Less than a week after the catastrophe, the firm of Frank O. Abbott and Son, owners of the hotel property as well as some 6,000 acres in the notch, announced that they would not rebuild and that the "little Yosemite" was for sale for the then-staggering price of $400,000.

The loss of the Profile House may have brought to a close an era of palatial hospitality in Franconia Notch, but it did not end the tourist trade there, for in 1924 more than 100,000 visitors paid 25¢ each to visit the Flume. Now, with lumber companies bidding for the standing timber, many of those same people would be asked to join with the Society for the Protection of New Hampshire Forests and the state to save the Old Man and the spectacular valley he watched over. Led by the SPNHF's forester Philip Ayres, the campaign to raise funds to buy the notch received nationwide publicity, especially after Ayres announced that trees would be "sold" by subscription for a dollar each and that the notch, once preserved, would be dedicated as a memorial to the men and women who

141

The Appalachian Mountain Club's Pinkham Notch Camp dates from 1920. The sign lists the Camp as a "Centre of Tramping and Skiing in the White Mountain National Forest."

had served the nation in times of war. Ayres's tactics, which included a widely circulated composite photo showing the Old Man peering out on a devastated forest, were ingenious and donations from some 15,000 contributors, ranging from $200,000 from the state legislature to $20 from an orphanage, allowed the Abbott Company's June 1, 1928, deadline to be met. In September, at official ceremonies held on the shore of Profile Lake, Franconia Notch became a "Forest Reservation and Memorial Park."

Before the mid-1920s, getting around in the White Mountains during winter meant taking a train or braving the elements behind horse-drawn sleighs on snow-covered roads packed down with heavy wooden rollers. The easy mobility provided by the automobile and growing popularity of such diverse cold weather activities as snowshoeing, ice skating, tobogganing, and dog sled racing served as incentives for the improvement of highways for winter travel. Thus, by 1930 snowplows were winning the battle against Mother Nature and, for the first time, people could drive their own cars through the rugged beauty of the formerly isolated notch areas. In Pinkham Notch, on Mount Washington's "Eastern Slope," visitors to the Appalachian Mountain Club's Trading Post were welcomed after 1922 by Joe Dodge, manager of the club's hut system until 1959. Known to his many acquaintances as the "Mayor of Porky Gulch," Dodge influenced hiking and backcountry recreation in the White Mountains in numerous and profound ways. A leading promoter of downhill skiing in the area, Dodge helped organize many ski races in Tuckerman Ravine and directed innumerable mountain rescues during his long career in the mountains.

In 1932, Joe Dodge and a small party of weather enthusiasts, including Robert Monahan, Alexander McKenzie, and Salvatore Pagliuca, joined forces to permanently reoccupy the summit of Mount Washington for the purpose of continuous meteorological observations. Stirred to action by the 1932–1933 International Polar Year Commission's focus on Arctic research, and inspired by the United States Signal Service's presence on the mountaintop from 1871–1892, these men, with support from the Cog Railway and Auto Road, were the founders of the Mount Washington Observatory. Today, it maintains the only continuously staffed mountaintop weather station in the western hemisphere. This valuable scientific facility made use of the Auto Road Stage Office until 1938, when it moved into what was then said to be "the strongest wooden building in the world," a two-story structure made of bridge timbers bolted to the underlying bedrock.

On April 12, 1934, while in the earlier location, the Observatory crew measured the highest winds ever recorded on Earth as they raced over the peak at an incredible 231 miles per hour. On that fateful day, staff members Alexander McKenzie, Salvatore Pagliuca, and Wendell Stephenson huddled inside the small, chained-down Stage Office, not knowing whether the ice-encrusted walls would give way at any second. The now famous anemometer used to measure the record wind is on display in the Observatory's Summit Museum, first opened to the public in 1973. Long known for its aviation research programs, icing studies, and weather observations, the Mount

The highest winds ever recorded on Earth—231 miles per hour—were measured on April 12, 1934, by the staff of the Mount Washington Observatory, then headquartered in the Carriage Road Stage Office.

CCC workers cut many downhill ski trails in the White Mountains during the 1930s. Two men take time out for lunch at the Summit Cabin on the Wildcat Trail.

Washington Observatory today offers a vastly expanded agenda of scientific and educational programs and activities revolving around its facilities in both the Sherman Adams Summit Building atop the mountain and the Weather Discovery Center at North Conway.

The stock market crash of 1929 and the ensuing Great Depression slowed the North Country economy, especially in such manufacturing centers as Berlin, where the number of jobs available in the pulp and paper industry plummeted. As conditions worsened, residents of rural communities throughout the White Mountains tightened their belts and made do or did without. "There was a strong Yankee tradition of thrift, ingenuity, and living within one's means," wrote the Honorable Margaret Joy Tibbetts, who was then living in Bethel, Maine, some 25 miles downriver of Berlin. "Many men were experienced in combining a bit of farming, lumbering and odd jobs on a regular basis. . . . In one way or another a good number of local people had several skills and were used to scrabbling for jobs."

One of the few bright spots during this season of fiscal calamity and economic dislocation was the creation of the Civilian Conservation Corps (CCC) in 1933, during the first term of President Franklin Roosevelt. One of several public works programs designed to put the nation's unemployed back to work, the CCC established more than a dozen encampments in the White Mountains and undertook numerous projects there designed to benefit the traveling public. In addition to cutting many of the region's earliest downhill ski trails (e.g. the Richard Taft Trail on Cannon Mountain, the John Sherburne Trail on Mount

144

Washington, and the Wildcat Trail on Wildcat Mountain), CCC workers improved or developed the Dolly Copp Campground, the Glen Ellis Falls Scenic Area, Moose Brook State Park at Gorham, the U.S. Forest Service Shelter at Hermit Lake in Tuckerman Ravine, and the Bear Notch and Evans Notch Roads.

Until the 1930s, skiing in northern New England consisted almost entirely of cross-country or jumping, "Nordic" techniques introduced in the late-nineteenth century when large numbers of Scandinavians settled in the region. In the White Mountains, Norwegian immigrants came to the city of Berlin in the 1880s to work in the woods for the Brown Company, and there organized the Nansen Ski Club to promote these winter sports, especially among young people. Named for Arctic explorer Dr. Fridtjof Nansen, this pioneering ski association brought Berlin tremendous prestige before World War II as the foremost ski-jumping center in the East. In addition, it was largely because of the club's presence that some of the earliest winter carnivals in the White Mountains took place in Berlin and the neighboring town of Gorham, beginning around 1920. During the 1932 Winter

Tuckerman Ravine's steep headwall was the scene of several "Inferno" races in the 1930s. In 1939, Toni Matt amazed onlookers by "schussing" the headwall without making any turns.

145

Olympics at Lake Placid, the United States was represented by two Nansen Club members. Six years later, the club again received national attention when it erected the "World's Largest Ski Tower" on the Milan Road north of Berlin. Outdated and falling into disrepair today, this huge steel ski jump was utilized during tryouts for the 1940 Olympic Games, which had to be canceled because of the onset of World War II.

The origins of downhill skiing or "controlled ski running" in the White Mountains extend back to several unsuccessful attempts made between 1899 and 1911 to scale Mount Washington on skis via the Auto Road and then descend by the same route to the Glen House. Members of the Dartmouth Outing Club, founded in 1910, finally achieved this objective in 1913, though not without difficulty on the icy, wind-swept slopes above the treeline. A year later, John S. Apperson of Schenectady, New York, became the first person to venture into the bowl of Tuckerman Ravine on skis. While many winter visitors during this era

The White Mountains are today home to numerous ski areas, snowboarding parks, and cross-country centers. From Waterville Valley in the west to Sunday River in the east, the region abounds in winter sports activity.

were content to glide through the hilly pasturelands available all over the White Mountains, more adventuresome skiers (including many Appalachian Mountain Club members) followed Apperson's lead and headed for that huge glacial bowl on the east side of Mount Washington, thus establishing a ritual of spring skiing for which Tuckerman is known worldwide.

In the early days of "Alpine" skiing in the region, little attention was paid to style, but this situation changed in 1929 when Austrian-born Sig Buchmayr established the first organized ski school in the United States at Peckett's on Sugar Hill, a resort community situated on a ridge above Franconia Village. By the early 1930s, a steady stream of winter devotees were pouring into the mountains on special "Snow Trains" from Boston's North Station, and later from New York City. Ski races on the Auto Road and down the headwall of Tuckerman Ravine (site of the first giant slalom race in the United States in 1937) brought many of America's top-ranking skiers, as well as large crowds of onlookers, to the White Mountains. Besides generating income for local stores and inns, such activities acted as an effective antidote to the general uneasiness brought on by the Great Depression.

The arrival of a number of mostly German and Austrian immigrants from the European Alps just before World War II enlivened ski instruction in the White Mountains. This was particularly apparent in the area around North Conway, where the Eastern Slope Ski School (an American branch of the famed Hannes Schneider Ski School in Austria) was established in 1936 in Jackson by Carroll Reed, founder of one of the first specialty ski shops in New England located slopeside rather than in an urban setting.

To provide the best in instruction and for publicity purposes, Reed hired Austrian Benno Rybizka to teach the perfect "Arlberg technique." In 1939, Hannes Schneider himself was brought to North Conway by Harvey Dow Gibson, whose financial resources and political maneuverings liberated the talented Austrian from house arrest by the Nazis in Germany. Until his death in 1955, Schneider was Skimeister at Mount Cranmore, where Gibson's unique Skimobile carried tens of thousands up the 1,690-foot mountain between 1938 and 1989.

By the late 1930s, skiing had become big business in the White Mountains, thanks in part to the development of various mechanisms for transporting people safely to the top of the slopes. Rope tows and T-bars were the first devices used, followed by one-person chairlifts. In Jackson, Betty and Bill Whitney improved an existing rope tow on the former Moody Farm by attaching shovel handles, thus creating one of the earliest overhead ski lifts in the East. The culmination of ski area development before the war came in late June 1938, when the Cannon Mountain Aerial Tramway—the first of its kind in North America—opened in Franconia Notch. This state-sponsored project, replaced in 1980 by "Tram II" which features larger, 80-passenger cars, proved to be as popular with warm weather visitors to this famous White Mountain peak as with skiers, a fact that remains true to this day.

During the five years America was immersed in World War II, skiing and other recreational activities were temporarily put on hold as the country's attention was diverted elsewhere. Far removed from the more vulnerable coastline, towns in the White Mountains were nevertheless drawn into the war effort as young men and women left to work in factories outside of the region or enlisted for military duty at home or overseas. While the Army and Navy conducted cold weather tests on various types of equipment atop Mount Washington, a number of local men who had learned "extreme skiing" on the sheer cliffs in Tuckerman Ravine soon found themselves part of the famed 10th Mountain Division, which trained in the Colorado Rockies and saw service in Italy and the Aleutian Islands.

As the war progressed, citizens in the valley communities of northern New Hampshire and westernmost Maine watched the skies from observation posts, and kept an eye on the area's important highway and railroad bridges to prevent sabotage. An increase in wartime freight traffic required as many as four "pusher" steam engines to get the trains up the steep mountain grade in Crawford Notch, much to the delight of photographers and rail fans.

In 1944, international attention was once again focused on the White Mountains when the "Bretton Woods Monetary Conference" was held at the newly refurbished Mount Washington Hotel. For three weeks, starting on July 1, financiers from 44 countries met in what was later termed "the first 'postwar' conference to be held anywhere in the world." This historic gathering, as a marker near the hotel now proclaims, "established the World Bank, set the gold standard at $35 an ounce, and chose the American dollar as the backbone of international exchange." Inside the hotel today is a bronze plaque designating "The Gold Room" where documents were signed giving the postwar world a badly needed currency stability.

When America's consumer-oriented society returned to the White Mountains in record numbers following the end of World War II, it was clear that the region's popularity as one of the country's top resort destinations had not diminished. On a daily basis during both summer and winter, larger and faster automobiles brought thousands of visitors to the North Country, where the long tradition of grand hotel hospitality had nearly vanished by the early 1960s as motels cropped up in every town and along every highway. It was also during this time that the long-standing struggle between conservation and commercial interests in the mountains again flared up at Franconia Notch, where pressure to build a four-lane interstate highway through the spectacular pass initiated a second campaign to "Save the Notch."

With the natural charms and extraordinary beauty of this unique natural environment at stake, sides were taken as a protracted legal battle ensued between the New Hampshire Highway Department and the White Mountain Environment Committee, chaired by Paul Bofinger, who was then president of the SPNHF. In the end, plans for a superhighway that would have required filling in parts of Profile and Echo Lakes, and perhaps damaging the Old Man of the Mountain, were abandoned and a two-lane parkway that preserved the heart of

During the 1960s and 1970s, a proposal to construct a four-lane interstate through Franconia Notch caused much debate. This unusual winter view of about 1920 shows the second Profile House and Echo Lake.

the notch was built instead. Construction of the parkway and the paralleling 8-mile paved Franconia Notch Recreation Trail commenced in 1978 and was completed nine years later.

Over the past half century, the impact of human activity on the White Mountains has continued to alter the landscape as well as change people's perceptions of the region, for the grand cathedral district of Thomas Starr King's day remains a physical place as well as a state of mind. Surrounded by civilization and bisected by some of New England's busiest highways, the White Mountains were subdued long ago. Today, condominium developments and strip malls have been substituted for the grand hotels and village general stores of an earlier era. And yet the sense of untamed wilderness that attracted millions to this corner of the Earth over the past 400 years has not entirely vanished, and thankfully neither have all the great hotels from the Golden Age, as the recently reopened 145-room Mountain View House in Whitefield testifies.

Home to a 1,200-mile network of hiking paths, including the most rugged section of the Appalachian Trail, these mountains still have the ability to challenge visitors, especially those who venture above the timberline on Mount Washington and other high peaks during adverse weather conditions. In an effort to protect and preserve the natural qualities of particularly outstanding sections of the White Mountain National Forest, some 115,000 acres—about 15 percent of the area—have been set aside as "Wilderness Areas" where logging,

149

Among the handful of grand hotels still operating in the White Mountains is the "Mountain View Grand" at Whitefield. Closed in the 1980s, this sprawling complex has reopened following a complete refurbishment.

road building, or the use of any type of mechanized vehicles are prohibited. Five such areas, made possible by a 1964 act of Congress, now exist within the confines of the Forest: the Pemigewasset Wilderness (45,000 acres), the Presidential–Dry River Wilderness (27,380 acres), the Sandwich Range Wilderness (25,000 acres), the Caribou–Speckled Mountain Wilderness (12,000 acres), and the Great Gulf Wilderness (5,552 acres), which was the first (1964) section of the mountains to be so designated.

The rich history of the White Mountain area of New Hampshire and Maine is in many respects the story of America itself. First explored by Europeans only a few years after they landed on this continent's shores, these mountains have loomed large in the public mind, so that many of the names and events chronicled in this modest volume have ceased to be of only regional importance and are now part of the nation's heritage. For the future of these ancient hills, change will most certainly remain constant. Within that continuum, finding ways to preserve an extremely fragile natural environment while allowing for such economic mainstays as tourism, manufacturing, and outdoor recreation will pose a daunting task. In the 1896 edition of his book *The White Mountains: A Guide to Their Interpretation*, Julius H. Ward wrote:

> The joy of being in the mountains is that every unused or waiting faculty
> of our higher nature is strained to the utmost to interpret them in the
> language of the spirit. . . . Great as is this gift to some, the use of the

mountains to lift us into the higher moods of life is common to us all. Like the air and the sky and the clouds and the sunlight, no one can lay exclusive claim to them. The unlikeness begins in the fitness of the spirit to interpret them.

Written more than a century ago, Ward's Ruskinian commentary is still relevant today, and serves to remind us of the continuing need to preserve a sense of "wildness" here as we celebrate and savor these enduring highlands—the Alps of New England.

Frankenstein Trestle, White Mountains, N. H.

One of the newest of the region's attractions is Conway Scenic Railroad's excursion through Crawford Notch and across Frankenstein Trestle. Regular service on the former Maine Central Mountain Division ended in 1983.

BIBLIOGRAPHY

Abbott, Karl P. *Open for the Season*. Garden City, NY: Doubleday & Company, Incorporated, 1950.

Allen, E. John B. *Images of America: New England Skiing, 1870-1940*. Dover, NH: Arcadia Publishing, 1997.

Ball, Benjamin L. *Three Days on the White Mountains: Being the Perilous Adventure of Dr. B.L. Ball on Mount Washington During October 25, 26, and 27, 1855*. Boston, MA: Nathaniel Noyes, 1856.

Bardwell, John D., and Ronald P. Bergeron. *The White Mountains: New Hampshire*. Norfolk, VA: The Donning Company/Publishers, 1989.

Barrows, John Stuart. *Fryeburg, Maine: An Historical Sketch*. Fryeburg, ME: Pequawket Press, 1938.

Beals, Charles Edward. *Passaconaway in the White Mountains*. Boston, MA: Richard G. Badger, 1916.

Belcher, C. Francis. *Logging Railroads of the White Mountains*. Boston, MA: Appalachian Mountain Club, 1980.

Billings, Marland P., Katherine Fowler-Billings, Carleton A. Chapman, Randolph W. Chapman, and Richard P. Goldthwait. *The Geology of the Mt. Washington Quadrangle, New Hampshire*. Concord, NH: State of New Hampshire Department of Resources and Economic Development, 1979.

Brown, Dona. *Inventing New England: Regional Tourism in the Nineteenth Century*. Washington, DC, and London, UK: Smithsonian Institution Press, 1995.

Burt, F. Allen. *The Story of Mount Washington*. Hanover, NH: Dartmouth Publications, 1960.

Calloway, Colin G. *The Abenaki*. New York, NY: Chelsea House Publishers, 1989.

———., ed. *Dawnland Encounters: Indians and Europeans in Northern New England*. Hanover, NH, and London, UK: University Press of New England, 1991.

Campbell, Catherine H., with Marcia Schmidt Blaine. *New Hampshire Scenery: a dictionary of nineteenth-century artists of New Hampshire mountain landscapes*. Canaan, NH: Phoenix Publishing, 1985.

Champney, Benjamin. *Sixty Years' Memories of Art and Artists*. Woburn, MA: By the Author, 1900.

Crawford, Lucy, ed. Sterns Morse. *The History of the White Mountains, from the First Settlement of Upper Coos and Pequaket*. Boston, MA: Appalachian Mountain Club, 1978.

Daniell, Gene, and Jon Burroughs, comp. and ed. *Appalachian Mountain Club White Mountain Guide*, 26th ed. Boston, MA: Appalachian Mountain Club, 1998.

Downs, Virginia C. *Life by the Tracks: when passenger trains steamed through the notch*. Canaan, NH: Phoenix Publishing, 1983.

Drake, Samuel Adams. *The Heart of the White Mountains: Their Legend and Scenery*. New York, NY: Harper & Brothers, 1881.

Foster, Michael K., and William Cowan, eds. *In Search of New England's Native Past: Selected Essays by Gordon M. Day*. Amherst, MA: University of Massachusetts Press, 1998.

Gosselin, Guy A., and Susan B. Hawkins. *Among the White Hills: The Life and Times of Guy L. Shorey*. Portsmouth, NH: Peter E. Randall Publisher, 1998.

Gove, Bill. *J.E. Henry's Logging Railroads: The History of the East Branch & Lincoln and Zealand Valley Railroads*. Littleton, NH: Bondcliff Books, 1998.

Hancock, Frances Ann Johnson. *Saving the Great Stone Face: the chronicle of the Old Man of the Mountain*. Edited by Ruth Ayres-Givens. Canaan, NH: Phoenix Publishing, 1984.

Hitchcock, Charles H., and others. *Mount Washington In Winter, or The Experiences of a Scientific Expedition Upon the Highest Mountain in New England, 1870-71*. Boston, MA: Chick and Andrews, 1871.

Hounsell, Janet McAllister, and Ruth Burnham Davis Horne. *Conway, New Hampshire 1765-1997*. Portsmouth, NH: Peter Randall Publisher, 1998.

Howe, Nicholas. *Not Without Peril: 150 Years of Misadventure on the Presidential Range of New Hampshire*. Boston, MA: Appalachian Mountain Club, 2000.

Johnson, Ron, ed. *Maine Central R.R. Mountain Division*. South Portland, ME: 470 Railroad Club, 1986.

Joslin, Richard S. *Sylvester Marsh and the Cog Railway*. Mount Washington, NH: Mount Washington Railway Company, 2000.

Julyan, Robert, and Mary Julyan. *Place Names of the White Mountains*. Revised edition. Hanover, NH, and London, UK: University Press of New England, 1993.

Keyes, Donald D., Catherine H. Campbell, Robert L. McGrath, and R. Stuart Wallace. *The White Mountains: Place and Perceptions*. Hanover, NH, and London, UK: University Press of New England, 1980.

Kidder, Glen M. *Railway to the Moon*. Littleton, NH: By the Author, 1969.

Kilbourne, Frederick W. *Chronicles of the White Mountains*. Boston, MA, and New York, NY: Houghton Mifflin Company, 1916.

King, Thomas Starr. *The White Hills: Their Legends, Landscape, and Poetry*. Boston, MA: Crosby, Nichols and Company, 1859.

Kostecke, Diane M., ed. *Franconia Notch: an in-depth guide*. Concord, NH: Society for the Protection of New Hampshire Forests, 1975.

Lansing, Lydia. *Jackson Skiing Legends: Celebrating 50 Years of Organized Skiing, 1936-1986*. Jackson, NH: Jackson Resort Association, 1986.

Leich, Jeffrey R. *Over the Headwall: A Short History of Skiing in Tuckerman Ravine*. Franconia, NH: New England Ski Museum, 1999.

McGrath, Robert L. *Gods in Granite: The Art of the White Mountains of New Hampshire*. Syracuse, NY: Syracuse University Press, 2001.

————, and Barbara J. MacAdam. *"A Sweet Foretaste of Heaven": Artists in the White Mountains, 1830-1930*. Hanover, NH, and London, UK: University Press of New England, 1988.

Monahan, Robert S. *Mount Washington Reoccupied: The Experiences of a Scientific Expedition Upon the Highest Mountain in New England, 1932-33*. Brattleboro, VT: Stephen Daye Press, 1933.

Oakes, William. *Scenery of the White Mountains: with Sixteen Plates from the Drawings of Isaac Sprague*. Boston, MA: Wm. Crosby and H. P. Nichols, 1848.

Pote, Winston. *Mount Washington in Winter: Photographs and Recollections, 1923-1940*. Camden, ME: Down East Books, 1985.

Purchase, Eric. *Out of Nowhere: Disaster and Tourism in the White Mountains*. Baltimore, MD, and London, UK: The Johns Hopkins University Press, 1999.

Spaulding, John H. *Historical Relics of the White Mountains*. Boston, MA: Nathaniel Noyes, 1855.

Sweetser, M.F. *The White Mountains: A Handbook for Travellers*. Boston, MA: James R. Osgood and Company, 1876.

Tolles, Bryant F., Jr. *The Grand Resort Hotels of the White Mountains: A Vanishing Architectural Legacy*. Boston, MA: David R. Godine, 1998.

―――. *Summer Cottages in the White Mountains: The Architecture of Leisure and Recreation, 1870 to 1930*. Hanover, NH, and London, UK: University Press of New England, 2000.

Trigger, Bruce G., ed. *Handbook of North American Indians*. Volume 15, *Northeast*. Washington, DC: Smithsonian Institution, 1978.

True, Nathaniel Tuckerman, ed. Randall H. Bennett. *The History of Gorham, New Hampshire*. Bethel, ME: R. H. Bennett, 1998.

Waterman, Laura, and Guy Waterman. *Forest and Crag: A History of Hiking, Trail Blazing, and Adventure in the Northeast Mountains*. Boston, MA: Appalachian Mountain Club, 1989.

Wight, D.B. *The Wild River Wilderness*. Littleton, NH: Courier Printing Company, Incorporated, 1971.

Willey, Benjamin G. *Incidents in White Mountain History*. Boston, MA: Nathaniel Noyes, 1856.

INDEX

The Society for the Protection of New Hampshire Forests operated the Flume from 1928 to 1947. This geological wonder remains a highly popular attraction in Fraconia Notch State Park.